HUNGRY

At the End of
Epi

Richard Acland

Dear Monica
Happy Christmas 1988
Lots of love
Alistair
xxx.

Marshall Pickering

Marshall Morgan and Scott
Marshall Pickering
3 Beggarwood Lane, Basingstoke, Hants RG23 7LP, UK

First published in 1988 by Marshall Morgan and Scott Publications Ltd
Part of the Marshall Pickering Holdings Group
A subsidiary of the Zondervan Corporation

ISBN 0–551–01613–2

Phototypeset in Linotron Caledonian by
Input Typesetting Ltd, London
Printed in Great Britain by
Cox & Wyman Ltd, Reading, Berks.

Contents

"The Hungry Sheep look up and are not fed."

John Milton in *Lycidas*, 1637.

"The convulsions of our English Church itself, grievous as they are, seem to be as nothing beside the danger of its calm and unobtrusive alienation in thought and spirit from the great silent multitude of Englishmen, and again of alienation from fact and love of fact; mutual alienations both."

F.J.A. Hort, theologian and New Testament scholar, in a letter to Archbishop Benson in 1882; quoted by S.C. Carpenter in *Church and People* (Seraph 1959), pp. 568/9

Personal Introduction

Those who have ever heard of me are almost all over fifty, and most of them are probably over sixty-five. I should like younger people to know what course of activity and experience can justify my writing a book of this kind. At one end of the track there is a religionless Liberal candidate; at the other a Socialist (or — as I would prefer to say — a believer in the Common Ownership Community) who is convinced that there can be no creative future for us except through a New Reformation, which will disturb many of the dwindling and ageing company of church-goers just as the earlier Reformation hurt the bishops and the cardinals and the Pope in the 1500s. As well as establishing my credentials — such as they are — I should like to set out the order of events through which the basic ideas of this book have developed in my mind. This will have an incidental and almost technical advantage. At more than a score of places in the main argument I shall be able to put my point in context with no more than a three-word footnote referring to this Introduction where otherwise there would have been needed four or five attention-losing lines so as to explain what was being discussed.

In middle adolescence I threw over religion with a four-stage argument: 'You Christians say that God exists; you ought to be able to prove it; I attend and you prove nothing; so there is no God'. I became a Humanist like most of our century's 'Do-Gooders'; and the contempt attached to the phrase now suggests that Humanism is not tough enough for the job in hand.

From as early as I can remember, it was taken for granted that I should follow family tradition and become a Liberal MP; I set off towards that goal with a minimum of serious thought. For example, R. H. Tawney wrote *Acquisitive Society* while I was at Oxford; but I did not bother to read it. In spite of that, after two earlier failures, I was elected for North Devon in 1935. This, and marriage to Anne Alford, seemed to bring me to life. I even started to read books, including *The General Theory* by J. M. Keynes, which converted me to Socialism, in effect by a single sentence:

> When the capital development of a country becomes a by-product of the activities of a casino the job is likely to be ill done.[1]

Today, when our industrial investment has been flagging while the City has manipulated paper property through computer screens, the sentence seems even truer than when Keynes wrote it.

I could honourably keep quiet about my conversion because, in those days, nothing mattered except Collective Security which I had advocated since the Japanese attack on China in 1931. This was the campaign to halt aggressors, while they were still few and weak, by the immense power which the League of Nations could have mobilised under resolute British leadership. The wretched descent into 'Unnecessary War'[2] was illuminated for me by a sharp experience one night on the sands of Croyde Bay which was part of my constituency. It was not Richard Acland having a new idea — a process with which I was familiar. It was an imperative from outside which in words could have been: 'People don't need your pandering promises.

[1] *Op. cit:* (Macmillan, 1936) p. 159.

[2] The name given to it by Churchill. *The Second World War* (Cassell, 1948) p. viii or ix.

Tell them that if they want peace and better times they need to be better people.' Since then I have increasingly believed that evil causes will win unless moral force is effectively deployed against them — a belief that has found little support through the century in which I have lived.

Outbreak of war ended the campaign for Collective Security and by February 1940 I declared my belief in Common Ownership in a Penguin Special called *Unser Kampf* to which the public response was astonishing. The book attempted some kind of linkage between politics, morality, economics and religion. But what sort of linkage? We never worked it out. Was it the need for profound social change so as then to bring forth more moral people; or did we first need to change the people so as to improve the structure of society? Despite persisting ambiguity, by 1942 we had established Common Wealth — an emergent political Party advocating Common Ownership of land and all major resources, not to make anyone better off, but to serve as the basis for a more morally directed way of life. For this policy we won sensational by-elections against Coalition candidates through the last three years of the war. Long afterwards, in a deeply researched book, Angus Calder wrote that

> The war was fought with the willing brains and hearts of the most vigorous elements in the community, the educated, the skilled, the bold, the active, the young, who worked more and more consciously towards a transformed post-war world.[3]

We did not create this hope; it was there in the air that people breathed. We expressed it more aggressively than others.

Even before the formation of Common Wealth, I had been recalled to a religious way of life through reading

[3] *The People's War* (Jonathan Cape, 1969) p. 18.

Good God by 'John Hadham'[4]. He was the first who positively told me that God is unprovable, not because Christians are incompetent, but because people are meant to be free. The book was quickly followed by a second external imperative which left me in no doubt. I began to read religious books amongst which I came upon *The Varieties of Religious Experience* by William James and *The Significance of Jesus* by W. R. Maltby. These both play their part in the book that now follows. During the same period I was deeply impressed by a single sentence from E. H. Carr whose message we ignore today at our peril:

> Our civilisation is in danger of perishing for lack of something with which we have dispensed for 200 years, but with which we can dispense no longer: a deliberate and avowed moral purpose, involving the call for common sacrifice for a recognised common good.[5]

Labour's landslide victory in 1945 left no serious alternative but to wind up Common Wealth and advise our supporters to join the Labour Party as individual members.

In the late summer of 1947, while Labour's reforming zeal was still in full spate, the Conservatives won nationwide local government gains by belly-aching. 'You haven't had much material reward for your great victory, have you?' In November, when the Labour MP for Gravesend was expelled from the House of Commons, everyone expected the Government's first by-election defeat. But I held the seat with the slogan: 'Tough Times: So What?'

By the early 1950s, 'Butskellism'[6] was draining all moral content out of politics. General elections became contests in which both sides competed for the floating voters with: 'Look! We will make you better off quicker than those

[4] Penguin 1940 and SCM 1966. See particularly pp. 33 *et seq* in the Penguin edition. 'John Hadham' was the pen name for the Reverend Dr James Parkes.

[5] *Conditions of Peace* (Macmillan, 1942) p. 111.

[6] An amalgamation of the names of R. A. Butler and Hugh Gaitskell to describe the common search for the middle ground.

others.' It was a contest in which ultimately Labour was bound to lose. For a number of years I believed that the wartime hopes for a nobler kind of society could have been realised if only we had had more resolute and inspired Labour leadership. In other words, I then accepted a part of what the Militants of the 1980s still believe — that a great cause was let down by weak leaders. On this view, the need is only to manipulate the selection of tougher candidates so that the whole of Socialism shall be bashed through in a single Parliament. Strangely, I had stumbled on the real cause of Labour's failure several years earlier. Many people, I wrote, were asking the wrong question: 'What kind of organisation could be run successfully by the sort of people we were in 1939?' To this question I saw only one answer: 'No organisation of society could be run successfully by the sort of people we were in 1939.'[7] When the war was over, too many persisted as, or once more became, the same sort of people they had been before. That was why we failed; but I did not say so then. Almost forty years on, I am trying to write it now.

Through 1951–54 I closed my eyes to Labour's depressing pragmatism by absorbing myself in *War on Want* — the name of a booklet on which I worked with Harold Wilson. It was the first time the phrase was publicly used. Oxfam had not yet entered the field, and Christian Aid had not been started. The great hope came from 'Point Four' in President Truman's Inaugural in 1949: 'A bold new programme for the improvement and growth of under-developed areas.' The United Nations appointed an expert group which concluded that 'a 2 per cent increase in the per capita national incomes cannot be brought about without an annual capital import well in excess of $10 billions.'[8] Any competent banker could have known that the under-developed world could never repay a 'capital import' of more than ten billions a year. The phrase meant 'gifts'. What! *Give* poor countries ten billions per year? It

[7] *What it Will be Like* (Gollancz, 1942) p.7.

[8] *Measures for the Economic Development of Under-Developed Countries* (U.N., 1951.II. B2) p.79.

would have been 3 per cent of the rich world's gross national product. Not a very high price for a world quite different from the world we know today.

Our campaign was pathetic when compared to the challenge that we were trying to meet. But it was good enough for its message to be heard by anyone minded to listen. From first to last not a man or woman from among 'the Good and the Great' lifted a finger to help us. An intimation of our living in a sick society?

Since writing *Unser Kampf* I had doubted the wisdom of suggesting that Socialism would make us all materially better off; though at the time I saw this mainly as a consequence of establishing fair shares with the world's poor. In 1954 the prospect took on a new dimension when I read *The Challenge of Man's Future* by Harrison Brown.[9] So far as I know he was the first author who ever tried to quantify the planet's limited resources, and to warn us that quite soon we should have to stop guzzling its capital and learn to live on its income. I took the book to the next meeting of the Bevanites[10] suggesting that it offered a far firmer foundation for all that we wanted to do than did Anthony Crossland's belief that the word 'Socialism' actually meant equal opportunity, fair shares and full employment in a country sustained by ever booming Capitalism. They rejected my argument because they were far more deeply rooted in the Labour Movement than ever I had been. The movement had emerged just over half a century earlier for the one purpose of challenging the wicked material poverty of unskilled workers. It had become emotionally impossible for my colleagues to believe that politics could be about anything else except ordinary people getting richer and richer.

Early in 1955 Attlee proposed that the Parliamentary Labour Party should go along with Churchill's decision to make British Hydrogen Bombs. A few of us argued that Churchill should be vigorously opposed, but we were

[9] Secker & Warburg, 1954

[10] This was the mocking name given to the Keep Left Group when Aneurin Bevan joined us in 1951 after resigning from the Cabinet.

voted down by at least ten to one. I decided to resign from the Party and the House so as to fight a by-election on the issue; but, unfortunately for me, Churchill at last decided to stand down and Eden called a General Election in which no one noticed an isolated anti-nuclear candidate in a single constituency. I was lucky to save my deposit.

Having lost my seat in the House, I taught elementary maths and physics for four years at Wandsworth Comprehensive School. It is a proud boast that I sang in the Russell Burgess choir before it became famous.[11] The great advantage of the years at Wandsworth was that they just, but only just, allowed the generous Principal to accept me into the Education Department of St Luke's College of Education in January 1960.

Almost by chance one of my four first-year seminar groups always consisted of all the students who had offered history as their first main subject, and another of all who had offered religious education. While working with the historians, I learned that their secondary schools had offered them an inaccurate picture of English history through the last thousand years. A more accurate understanding will be offered in an early part of the book. It forms an important part of my argument.

With the R.E. students, I was surprised that the Education Department of a Church College should include, on its reading list, *An Introduction to the Philosophy of Education* by Professor D. J. O'Connor.[12] It offered almost nothing about education and almost everything about Logical Positivism which involves denial of religion in any possible form and repudiation of there being any meaning or purpose in human life on earth. This, like the wrong teaching of history, will need to be considered more closely at a later stage. At the time, I met O'Connor in

[11] Bach: St John's Passion. Decca Set 531/2/3. Schumann: Scenes from Faust. Decca Set 567/8.

[12] Published by Routledge & Kegan Paul in 1957. The publishers informed me that the book has sold in tens of thousands in Universities and Colleges.

public debate before a packed audience of students and tutors. His book was dropped from the reading list.

In the same years, with the same groups of R.E. students, I was thrilled by *Honest to God* which seemed to offer entirely new teaching opportunities. Those who were born later than in 1945 will hardly remember the explosion detonated by this little paperback, written by John Robinson, the Bishop of Woolwich, and published by SCM in March 1963. More than a million copies were sold in Britain in twelve months; the book was translated into at least seven languages. The orthodox vehemently condemned it; but many hundreds of people wrote to say that for the first time in their lives religion in general and Christianity in particular seemed to make sense and might be important.

By comparison it was very small beer that in May of the same year Gollancz published *We Teach Them Wrong* which arose from my having taken the weekly R.E. lesson with seventeen secondary modern fifth formers who stayed on for an extra year in the hope of O-level success. The book was quite well reviewed, went into three editions and produced no effect whatever.

From out of the turmoil produced by John Robinson's book, Canon Roger Lloyd wrote *Ferment in the Church*. Lloyd was Vice-Dean of Winchester and a typical middle-of-the-road churchman with no radical or revolutionary axe to grind. He wrote:

> We know now that the Church will never convert this country until it and its theology and its membership come out of the giant Ivory Tower in which we have too long been sheltering . . . That facts long known and recognised should all of a sudden pass from causing a dull ache, which is bearable, to a sharp pain, which is intolerable, can be explained only by an outburst of the awakening power of the Holy Spirit.[13]

[13] *Op. cit:* (SCM, 1964) pp. 15 & 13.

Lloyd wrote all this, and much else in the same sense, as if he were making judgments about which no competent observer could possibly disagree.

How did all this drain away leaving no more impact than a barrel of water spilled on the Sahara? The traditionalists were naturally delighted. They had been appalled by the prospect of real change; and no change was what happened. But what of the thoughtful churchmen in the middle? How did the sharp intolerable pain change back into the dull bearable ache? Robinson contributed to the outcome by doing nothing. But was there a deeper reason? This question brought back to me all that I had gained by association with Professor John Macmurray, a member of Common Wealth who was unconcerned with our week-to-week problems but was a guide on fundamental issues. In his book, *The Clue to History*[14] , he described the on-going conflict between Christianity understood as the eternal purpose of Jesus, and 'Christianity' as offered at any particular time by the institution that works in his name. It can be said that Macmurray's lifetime purpose was to distinguish between the dualistic thinking of the Greeks and the unitary thinking of the Hebrews. The Greeks, he held, could divorce thought from action; they could take one aspect of life — religion — and speculate whether it could be 'applied' to other aspects. To the Hebrews, life was a whole and every aspect of it *was* religion. Robinson seemed to have written from a Greek, or dualistic, point of view. He showed us how to look at religion in a twentieth-century way. But he hardly wrote a line which would help us to understand the twentieth century. In what follows I shall try to avoid making this mistake, even at the risk of being led into wrong guesses about the future.

Although I can now look back and ask questions about the death of *Honest to God*, the hopes stirred by the book persisted with me for a long time. Until after retirement from St Luke's in 1974, I still believed that a cooperation between radical church-goers and religious Humanists

[14] SCM, 1938.

could suffice for the reconstruction of man and society. No sharp memorable event changed this view. By the early 1980s I knew the uselessness of looking to untypical minorities when our whole people were being starved of the religious truth without which there can be no social creativity. I have been trying to write this book ever since.

An unexpected benefit from St. Luke's was my friendship with P. W. Martin, educational psychologist and frequent contributor to our 'trade union journal' *Learning for Teaching*. I drove across southern England for long discussions with him in Kent.

Looking at my whole activity and experience, it will be obvious that I am not a historian, not a scientist, not a theologian nor any other kind of scholar. I have lived my life as a communicator; and I make no complaint if someone says that I have been a propagandist. It is only in relatively recent times that the word has attracted its bad smell. But I claim to have been a contemplative communicator. I have constantly asked myself questions about my own work, and about other people's work, in communication or propaganda. When evil causes won the upper hand, or when good causes seemed to fail, I asked: What has happened to the people? What has gone wrong with the communicators? In this book I ask these questions about the Church whose good cause is so obviously failing to win the people; and about the people who are not being won. At the risk of making those wrong future guesses, I speculate about some of the major developments that might follow if our whole society were ever again to be possessed by a living religion attuned to our contemporary social condition.

Richard Acland, College,
Broadclyst, Exeter.

1

Diagnosis of a Sick Society

Of his patients in the second half of life, Carl Gustav Jung wrote that 'every one of them fell ill because he had lost that which the living religions of every age have given to their followers.' These patients, he said, were not 'sickly eccentrics' but most often exceptionally able courageous, and upright persons 'who had repudiated our traditional truths' for honest and decent reasons.[1] But what is a living religion?

A society can be permeated by a living religion without having complete and unalterable answers to all the deepest questions about human life. Remote tribes have been sustained by living religions making only rough approximations to ultimate reality. Very few of us — indeed very few of today's church-goers — could accept Christianity if it were offered with all the appurtenances which gathered around it eight hundred or four hundred years ago. Yet medieval and puritan Christianity served as living religions in their day because each then made a sufficiently good fit with the social state of their contemporaries. A society ceases to have a living religion when an unprecedented development in its knowledge and understanding is not matched by any comparable improvement in the way in which its religious leaders are offering the truth. The absence of a living religion not only brings increasing numbers of men and women, one by one, into the psychiatrists' consulting rooms. It also creates a psychologically sick society.

Recently — say from 1976 to 1987 — in one-to-one

[1] *Modern Man in Search of a Soul* (Kegan Paul, 1933) pp. 264, 268.

conversations I have many times put forward the proposition: 'We are now a psychologically sick society.' This has been offered, not as a throw away line, but as an opening for serious discussion; and quite often when someone else has taken the initiative by asking how I see our social situation. In all these conversations I was meeting intelligent and well-informed people; and hardly ever has any one of them responded with: 'Psychologically sick? Surely not. Basically we are quite all right.' Almost all accepted my judgment as a proper starting point for a consideration of the present state of our country. But it is fair to add that, in a Somerset village, a Church of England discussion group qualified their acceptance with 'not more sick than at some other times.'

In this situation it is surprising to find that our people are today divided into two main groups. Those in the smaller group are church-goers who appear to be outwardly content with the general message that now comes from the Church. (Here, and in all that follows, 'Church' is to mean institutionalised Christianity in all its denominations and sects.) The other and far larger group embraces those who watch the Church slowly dying on its feet with: 'What of it? Let it die. Who cares?'

The larger group is obviously unconcerned about religious truth. It is less clear that, in an important sense, the same is true of the *leaders* of the smaller group. Emphasis must be thrown on the leaders because I shall repeat several times that this book is not any kind of personal attack on the general company of church-goers. Most of them are making a genuine contact with spiritual truth in the services that they attend. Some of them are my personal friends; they seem to be, on average, better citizens than most of their secular neighbours. It is not morally wrong for people to live with a personal outlook — a personal *Weltanschauung* or world-view — much like that which was fairly general amongst their ancestors two, three or four generations ago. A case can be argued on behalf of priests and ministers in their parishes. Each, on arrival, meets the local church-goers who are the people for whom he has promised to care. It would need unusual courage to express the truth in ways that might seriously upset a good many of them.

The same excuses can hardly be offered for bishops or for the principals of theological colleges. Is it right that they should seem to concentrate their energy and their resources on the dwindling and ageing minorities who still go to church? Should they treat the unruffled month-to-month persistence of their own institution as their paramount concern? In the 1960s I had a vivid illustration of this paramountcy when an expensive theological quarterly published an article of almost unbelievable enlightenment written by one of our most forward-looking bishops — at that time a suffragan. I wrote to congratulate him and to beg him to have his article translated into language which could make his truth available, say, to the readers of the *Daily Mail*. His answer was quite unambiguous. In more than half of the parishes in his diocese, the work of the Church was being done by groups composed wholly or largely of Fundamentalists. The whole thing would be thrown into disarray if too many people knew too soon how their bishop was conceptualising religious truth in the twentieth century. From his point of view it would have been good, if possible, to make the truth available to the majority. The disarray of a diocese was too high a price to pay.

It is easy to sympathise with the bishop. Many years earlier he had learned and accepted Christian truth; like millions before him, he longed to light up the same truth in others; to this end he was ordained into the institution which has carried Christianity through almost two thousand years. Because of his abilities and personal characteristics he rose to become a bishop. The institution was responsible for his calling; he was responsible for a significant part of the institution. No matter for what high cause, was he to strike a destabilising blow in a diocese of the institution to which he was giving his life? It is a terrifying challenge; and in a like situation none can be sure that he would give the right answer.

Though we may sympathise with all bishops who face this awful choice, we have to think of the story of the lost sheep. Shepherds, it will be recalled, are expected to leave as many as 99 per cent of the flock so as to go and find out what has happened to as few as 1 per cent who are lost.[2] Today, on an optimistic estimate, the shepherds have hardly as many as 15 per cent in their folds. What of the far larger numbers who are 'lost'? There are three elements involved in religious teaching and religious learning. The first is the ultimate truth about human life which does not change. The second is the deep general outlook of the people which can change startlingly in as little as two or three generations. The third is *the way in which* the unchanging truth is being offered to the ever changing people.

No one can blame parish priests and ministers if pressing weekly business prevents them from giving serious time and energy to an analysis of the three interacting elements. But surely, somewhere in its institutional organisation, the Church should have gathered a team from amongst its wisest and profoundest and most up-to-date believers so as to keep continuous watch on the second of these two elements and to advise about changes needed in the third. As a small example, back in the 1930s, should not such a team have appointed a small group to meet Jung — and, if possible, some of his patients — so as to find out why exceptionally able, courageous and upright persons were rejecting traditional truths 'for honest and decent reasons'?[3] Instead of this, the leaders of the Church seem to have accepted an entity perceived as 'The Message' which would include established concepts, historical assertions, formulae, doctrines, creeds and much else; and then to have seen it as a prime duty of the Church to persist in the proclamation of their virtually sacrosanct 'Message' without bothering to find out whether it was still intelligible to the people. And then some of them seem to have

[2] Matthew 18.12.
[3] See p. 11 above.

blamed the people when 'The Message' was accepted by fewer and fewer. 'Do not seriously consider the people!' It does not sound like anything that would have come from Jesus.

In this situation, there is a personal question to be considered. *Why do I seem to be a freak?* Why do I seem to have so few companions who know that a living religion is a basic requirement for social good health; who see that a living religion is no longer reaching the people from the Church; and who therefore understand that on any long view the top social priority, bar none, is to puzzle out the new ways in which the unchanging truth about life might be effectively carried to the majority of our ever changing people? Why is not this essential task a matter of urgent concern in the Senior Common Room of every college and university in the land?

An answer emerges from the fact that most of us end our formal education with an inaccurate understanding of history, and relatively few learn better later on. This can be disastrous because our vision of the past profoundly affects our behaviour in the present and our hopes and intentions for the future. I know the general ideas with which we leave the top forms of our secondary schools because — as I have said already — through fourteen years at St Luke's College, one of my seminar groups consisted of students who had scored A-level success in history.

Most of us soon forget the details of the story; but almost all have a mental picture of the basic shape of what has happened. All my students had been taught that in the last thousand years there has been just the one great outburst of social creativity. It came at the dead end of the medieval period when the rediscovery of Greek intellect woke men from a superstition-laden sleep and brought forth the glorious Renaissance which gave our ancestors a new outlook, new art, new intellectual powers, scientific investigation, voyages of discovery and all the marvels of Individualism. In short, the Renaissance is accepted as the one great creative moment in our past. With this vision of history, religion looks like something from which we have to escape. What we seem to need is more intellect and more dynamic Individualism.

This way of understanding history is not wrong *because* it leads to unhappy conclusions. It is wrong because it is contrary to the facts. There has not been just the one great outburst of social creativity; there have been two.

2

The Historical Perspective

It would be an exaggeration to say that we know nothing at all about the first great outburst of social creativity. My students knew that from the eleventh century the medievals, with their feudal organisation of society, had been tough enough to keep out the marauding barbarians, and that they had built big castles and splendid cathedrals. But this, as they had learned it, was achieved at the cost of social stagnation and technological ossification under the power of a superstition-laden Church until the glorious onset of our modern age. Not one of my A-level students had been taught that the emergence of sufficient social stability in the eleventh century was preceded by the immense spiritual achievements of the tenth century. Not one perceived that the social structure of medievalism was different in kind from the structure of any large orderly society that had ever sustained itself for a few centuries in Europe or in any other part of the world. Not one had been taught that the early medieval centuries were pulsating with technological dynamism. Because these facts are left out of our secondary education, they must be considered for a moment here.

From before the collapse of Rome there had been bishops and priests and monks in western Europe. But, until the end of the tenth century, in no sense did they create or sustain the social conditions in which they lived. Some may have died comfortably in old age; but all knew that their monasteries, their little churches and the communities to which they ministered, could be destroyed at any time by the next influx of dynamic marauders. It was only through the immense spiritual achievement known as the Cluniac Revival that this sorry state of affairs was brought to an end at the opening of the eleventh century. R. H. Tawney, in *Religion and the Rise of Capitalism* wrote:

> the Church had been engaged in an immense missionary effort, in which, as it struggled with the surrounding barbarism, the work of conversion and of social construction had been almost indistinguishable.[1]

In passing, how very different were the Christians of those great days from some of our church-goers who would have agreed with the Reith Lectures offered by Edward Norman in 1978. He argued — as have many others — that religion is about nothing except saving individual souls and should not be at all concerned about the structure of society. It will have been seen that we shall return to this point later. For present purposes, I would commend the first two episodes in Sir Kenneth Clark's television series which were titled *By the Skin of our Teeth* and *The Great Thaw*. As the closing sentence in the first episode Clark said:

> By the year 1000, the long dominance of the barbarian wanderers was over and western Europe was prepared for its first great age of civilisation.

Early in the second episode, after a quick summary of the many-sided social creativity, he said:

> These changes imply a new social and intellectual background. They imply wealth, stability, technical skill and, above all, the confidence necessary to push through a long-term project. How had all this suddenly appeared in western Europe? Of course there are many answers, but one is overwhelmingly more important than the others: the triumph of the Church.[2]

[1] *Op. cit:* (Pelican edition, 1938) p. 34.
[2] The series is published as *Civilisation* as its overall title by BBC and John Murray (1969). My quotations are from pp. 31 & 34–5.

For sure, Clark treated the Church more as a power than as a faith. But if people had not been socially gripped by a living religion, they could not have put forth the cooperative effort needed to raise huge cathedrals and big churches in small cities and tiny villages when every stone had to be quarried, transported, shaped and lifted by muscle power. If they had not believed it personally then, however silly it may seem to us, they would not have left their land, whose management in those days usually equated with local government, so as to make the arduous journey to Compostella, or to some other shrine, in the hope that contact with a holy relic would somehow save their souls.

I never knew that there was anything special about the structure of medieval society until 1944 when Professor George Trevelyan — a long-standing friend of the family — came to receive the title deeds of the Killerton and Holnicote estates on behalf of the National Trust. After the ceremony, I asked him about medievalism and, by aerial gestures, 'drew' a diagram of the chain of authority. At the top was the king; under him the dukes; then the barons, lords of the manors, knights and finally the serfs. How was this different from Nebuchadnezzar with, under him, the satraps, the sub-satraps, the sub-sub-satraps so as finally to reach the cultivators in their fields? Trevelyan answered at once that the decisive difference lay in the location of power. In every previous large-scale civilisation, real power had been at the centre. If the sub-sub-sub satrap faced unusual local trouble, he had to go up the chain of authority and ask for a detachment of central power. By contrast, under the feudal system, power lay around the circumference. Kings had their body guards, of course. But when they needed real power to meet a grave emergency, they had to go down the chain of authority at the end of which the village lads were called to turn out and fight. For the first time in human history there was a social structure in which those who worked in the fields could believe that they were a needed part of the whole show. Perhaps the subsequent development of our political

Democracy was grounded as much in medievalism as in anything coming to us from Greece.

It was another twenty years before I read Lynn White's *Medieval Technology and Social Change*.[3] Windmills and water wheels — usually quite small ones — had been known in earlier times and other places. It was left to the medievals to make big ones and to apply them to some twenty or thirty productive processes. By the end of the period, many cities had their public clocks. Some of them showed the date and the state of the moon. On a few, knights chased dragons around the tower at nine, twelve, three and six. If we consider what this must have meant in shafts and cog-wheels, we may wonder whether the Industrial Revolution was not born in the medieval centuries. The rudder-guided ocean-keeping cannon-bearing ship was the supreme instrument through which the Europeans imposed themselves on the rest of the human race from the 1400s until the outbreak of the 'European Civil War' in 1914. Its sails and rudder bar were controlled through pulleys and running tackle which were themselves medieval inventions. The voyages of discovery, from the fifteenth century, owed everything to medieval technology and nothing to Greek intellect.

Medieval society and medieval creativity could not last for ever. This calls our attention to an overwhelmingly important fact which is far more obvious when it relates to the past in which we are not emotionally involved; and far more obscure when it affects the present which pervades our lives at every level. Social philosophies, unlike (say) roses and poison gas, are not good fullstops or bad fullstops wherever and whenever they occur. They have to be valued in relation to time and circumstances.

Even at the outset, medieval society offered much less than total security for all. There were international and civil wars, dukes fought each other for territorial expansion and private brigandage was widely practised. Towns and cities, and at times whole provinces, were destroyed or

[3] Published by OUP in 1962.

depopulated by these bloody activities. Some critics will suppose that this invalidates my whole argument; but they are wrong. It is unreasonable to expect that the first great age of Christian civilisation should eliminate all the rapacity of powerful men. It must be enough if it creates — as it did — 'the confidence necessary to push through a long-term project.' This confidence was sustained by Authority, which upheld a crude slogan: 'Born a baron, stay a baron; born a serf, stay a serf.' This would be wholly unacceptable in our day. But we must not, on that account, perceive it as wholly negative. Even on the lowest members of the social hierarchy, it conferred a sense of participating in an organic whole — something which is grimly lacking in the psychologically sick society of our day. Peasants in their fields knew that they were not the only kind of people who paused for a minute from their superficial business when they heard the angelus bell.

But it could not endure. At its inception it had been inspired by a living religion. Our starting point was that a living religion does not require a perfect and unalterable assertion of eternal truth. It needs no more than an assertion which makes a good fit with the social conditions of the time. This is what medieval Christianity had offered. Looking back on it from our day we can see that it involved a religious error far more serious than the simple fancy that souls were saved in people who touched holy relics. *It depended on Authority*. If people asked why they should believe it, they were told: 'Because the Church says so.' But Jesus said: 'Allow the children to come to me, and don't forbid them.'[4] He did not say: 'Compel the children to come to me, and don't allow them to go anywhere else.' In our day we can see that any worthy and effective religious faith must depend on the free and conscious decision of each separate believer. This was far less obvious at the end of the medieval period. The Church had once seemed like society's splendid shield; only gradually did it come to be felt more as a straightjacket. Once it had

[4] Luke 18.16.

sustained the Whole; only gradually was it perceived as an oppressor — and as a rather corrupt and money-grubbing oppressor at that. The whole structure had to be transcended. And it was. This was an epoch-making event in the accurate meaning of the much abused phrase. It made the epoch in which we live, though with a diminishing sense of confidence.

I have not timidly admitted, but have positively asserted, that I am not any kind of scholar. So I do not try to make uninformed guesses in an area where professional historians still disagree. Their common ground seems to be that our epoch emerged from many inter-weaving sources. Marxists, and their like, naturally stress the increase in wealth and the expansion of trade which had been made possible by the relative security of the medieval period. For many academics, the driving force will seem to come from the Renaissance, from the rediscovery of Greek learning, and from the consequent understanding that people, as well as having souls to be saved, have minds to be put to work in the situation where they live. For sure, the Marxists and the academics are offering a part of the truth. When this has been fully allowed, the religious power of the Reformation cannot be left out of account. Some of my students had learned that the Reformation itself was a product of the Renaissance. But this is *post hoc propter hoc* based on the fact that the Renaissance was well established in Italy by 1400 and that hardly anyone had heard of Luther before the 1520s. (The terse Latin words mean, roughly, that if B happens after A, then people will tend to think that A must have been the cause of B.) This won't do. Though suppressed by Authority for more than a hundred years, most of the beliefs of the Reformation had been asserted by John Wycliffe well before the end of the 1300s when English life had hardly been touched by any influence from classical Greece. Through the work of Lollard preachers, and through their occasional martyrdom, both the educated elite and the common people of England had been permeated by the new religious thinking long before Luther burned the Papal Bull in 1521.

Whatever the strange backward-and-forward-looking qualities of Luther's rhetoric, whatever (to us) the strange qualities of Calvin's argumentation, one basic fact stands out. People were to accept their religious faith, not by submitting to an authoritarian Church, but by their own individual understanding of the Bible.

We who live in a society which is saturated in Individualism may underestimate the greatness of the achievement. We forget that in 1500 people looked back and saw that all large civilisations had always been authoritarian. From time to time there had been almost mindless revolts against Authority when the poor could no longer tolerate the domination of the rich. With the emergence of Individualism, something new in kind was coming into the world. Professor John Macmurray wrote of it:

> Negatively it is a revolt against authority and as such it is no new thing . . . But it is not until the end of the Middle Ages in Europe that we find a general movement of human effort associated with a sense of rightness and widely supported by the conscience of the masses.[5]

Wherever the Renaissance made its impact, there were new men with new ideas, new sculpture, new pictures, new music, new architecture. But there was something far more important and far more difficult than any of these. There was the emergence of an entirely new kind of society with a new structure and a new motivation. This was not achieved wherever the Renaissance reached. It was achieved in parts of Europe, and in lands colonised by Europeans, where a new religion won the upper hand. This can be seen most clearly by looking at the outstanding contrasts. It is obvious beyond all possibility of doubt that by the early 1600s there was a vivid difference — a difference not in degree but in kind — between the structure

[5] *The Clue to History* (SCM, 1938) pp. 169–70.

and motivation of society in Massachusetts on the one hand and in Spain on the other. Different parts of Europe were spread out at different points along the continuum stretching between the two extremes; and the points at which they stood depended, not indeed wholly but very substantially, on the extent to which they had either freed themselves from the Authoritarians' religion or remained under its power. Even when new knowledge was discovered by Roman Catholics in Roman Catholic countries, its free and rapid dissemination often depended on the Reformation. For example, Andreas Vesalius (1514–1564) lived in Italy while he worked out the revolutionary improvements in our knowledge of anatomy which had been laid down by Claudius Galen in the second century AD, and taught by Authority ever since. He did this by scientific observation of details in the bodies of animals and humans who had recently died. But he went over the Alps with his manuscript, and with unprecedentedly clear woodcuts made for him by outstanding artists, so as to have his work published in Geneva where unlimited printing would be allowed. Galileo could have had a much easier time if he had followed the example. The point being made is that the marvellous outburst of Individualism surely had a whole tangle of related causes; but a major cause was the emergence of a living religion which made a good fit with the social state of its contemporaries. This does not mean that all the religious affirmations of those days can earn credence with people who will live, or with people whose children will live, into the twenty-first century.

In fact, in most of its various forms, the new religious outlook included a teaching which to almost all of us — even to almost all of today's church-goers — seems quite repulsive. It was the teaching of Predestination. Each, it was held, was *predestined* before birth to Heaven or Hell, and no subsequent behaviour could affect the outcome. If nothing could make any difference, one might expect that many would cheat at business, booze and womanise to the utmost possible extent. On the contrary, a majority of believers set out to show their neighbours that they belonged to God's elect. And this they did, with the drive of religious conviction, by unbelievably hard work, honesty in business and abstemious living. These were the men who created the economic age of Individualism with their crude slogan: 'Everyone work hard for his own self-interest.' With this slogan such men built up the privately owned bank balances some of which made an indispensable contribution to the Industrial Revolution. Indeed the Industrial Revolution would have been impossible if the men of the day had not been freed from the shackles of government control so as to drive the thing through with their individual initiatives. The American and the French Revolutions, and our own slower and less violent movement towards political Democracy, could not have happened except among people who were permeated by Individualism.

These material and political facts seem less important when set against the spiritual value of Individualism in its early creative period. It was religiously necessary to escape from Authoritarianism. Separate men and women had to know that human life is fundamentally different from the life of a herd of cows directed by the farmer. They had to learn that, on the greatest questions of life, human beings are meant to use their minds for themselves, to stand on their own feet, to make their own decisions about the kind of life they will try to live and to challenge accepted attitudes on the strength of nothing more than their own sincere convictions. For sure, the religious necessity involved appalling dangers. Freed from Authority, individuals and whole human societies might make their basic decisions wrongly. Perhaps they might even decide that the whole purpose of life is to accumulate as much material wealth as possible! Awareness of this danger must have contributed to the Counter-Reformation which was so successful in so many parts of Europe. At the time it would have seemed that there was no way of avoiding the dangers except by re-asserting Authority. On any long view it was the wrong way. Despite all the dangers, it remains religiously true that we are not fully human if we do not make our most important decisions for ourselves. And despite some of his less endearing characteristics, there is a certain grandeur about Luther: 'Here I stand. I can no other. So help me God.' It is a very trivial matter that I could not write this kind of book if I did not have five hundred years of Individualism behind me.

The material products and the social institutions of the age of Individualism are now all around us, and they make an almost endless display. There is one of them which embraces all the others and far exceeds the sum of their separate importance. Individualism created our industrial society. *But that's the problem!* How can our contemporary industrial society be managed? How can we afford all its members the dignity of work? How can we create and sustain in them any feeling of personal responsibility to contribute to the good health of the whole? How can we combine an acceptable sense of justice with a reasonable degree of freedom? How do we arrest and then reverse the trend to increasing crime and violence? How do we offer to thousands of young people something better than drugs? What do we do about our living in a society with sex on the brain which, as someone said, is a bad place to have it? Is it permanently acceptable that take-over bidders and other property manipulators, creating nothing and offering negligible employment to others, should scoop, in a few months, more than is earned in a lifetime's work, say, by a probation officer, and more than is earned in a year by someone near the top management of a major productive industry? How do we create, or restore to people, a sense of there being some kind of meaning and purpose in human life? How do we cope with the widespread sense of alienation which is accepted by so many writers as central to their discussions? How do we explain the fact that with far more material wealth than ever before, people do not seem to be happier than before — indeed rather the reverse? Twenty years ago from people over sixty, and quite recently from someone over eighty, I heard hair-raising memories of the poverty in which they lived their early years. At the time of our conversations, all these people were rich enough to own television sets; and yet our conversations almost always ended: 'Ah, but in those days, we were happy.' I do not believe that this is wholly due to their looking back through rosy spectacles.

These, and other questions which other people could suggest, constitute the all-embracing problem of contemporary industrial society. It seems intrinsically unlikely or, as some might say, flatly impossible that a problem on this scale can best be handled by an intensification of the Individualism which has brought it into being.

Our civilisation is more complex than was any previous civilisation; and within it far more people are more inextricably related to and dependent on far more other people than in any civilisation at any earlier time. If there were such a process as awarding 'marks' for complexity, relatedness and mutual dependence, and if all earlier tribes and societies scored from one to ten, then our industrial civilisation would have to be marked between a hundred and a thousand. And yet more than nine tenths of our best educated people — more than nine tenths of those who passed through our public schools and universities — make no audible public protest against the proposition that the best way to run such a society as ours is to have every man, woman and group flat out for his, her or its self-interest. I can think of no more persuasive evidence for my opening proposition: we are now a psychologically sick society. And the sickness is not welling up from the lower orders amongst whom it ought to be suppressed. It is trickling down on us from the most eminent, the most respectable, the most influential and the richest who so much enjoy a wrong attitude to life.

Among well educated people to whom I offered the theme of the last three paragraphs in the early and middle 1980s, far more than half switched off the discussion with some dismissive comment on the 'Other Political Parties'. This is escapism. It is a rationalisation of their emotional wish to stay on good terms with their influential friends. It is a confusion between Party Politics and Social Philosophy which are today only tenuously connected. Party Politics, as at present practised, is a 'this-year-next-year' attempt to put together a programme which could win an election *without any serious change in the outlook of the people.* Social Philosophy raises the question whether there is any chance of our living creatively and harmoniously through the next two centuries *unless people's general outlook is dramatically changed.*

To return to the basic theme of the present chapter, it must be repeated that they are wrong who look back on the last thousand years of European history and see only one creative social transformation. There have been two. Each emerged when there were enough people moved by a living religion — by an affirmation of eternal truth which fitted the social state of its contemporaries. Each led to an immense outburst of social creativity. Each came to its dead end after some four or five hundred years. The episode of Individualism has come to its dead end now.

This allows a comment on the frequent assertion that we cannot change human nature. No doubt this is true even though it is so often asserted by people who seem to be doing pretty well for themselves with human nature as it is. If there are to be changes in human nature, they will depend on millennia rather than on decades. This does not alter the fact that there can be dramatic changes in human outlook in much shorter periods. The outlook of the early medievals was sharply different from that of the wandering marauders who had been so dominant until only a few decades earlier. The outlook of the early religious Individualists was different on the same scale from that of the preceding Authoritarians. The religionless Individualists of our day have a very different outlook from their religious predecessors. Our human *nature* will not change. But that is no reason why there could not be a significant change in our outlook within a quite short time. On this basis there is at least an arguable case for my earlier proposition that on any long view our top social priority, bar none, is to puzzle out the ways in which the unchanging truth about life might be carried effectively to the majority of our ever changing people. This, I suggested, ought to be a cooperative endeavour undertaken by some of our ablest men and women. In this book I have to confront it with such abilities and experience as I have. If critics find gaps and errors, they will not prove that the work does not need to be done. They will prove only that others must try again where I fail.

There remains a verbal question. If ever we reach a more harmonious, less alienated and more socially creative future, what will be its name? This is a dicey question because epochs usually acquire their abiding names only after they have been working for quite a long time. But I must have an answer if only for the sake of the impending argument. I therefore tentatively suggest that the epoch may be described as the age of Wholism; and those who sustain it, as Wholists.

The words are offered so as to correct what may have been the most disastrous spelling mistake in the history of English writing. In the 1920s, the tragic unfolding of South Africa's story lay mostly in the future. Jan Smuts, South African Premier, had been our enemy in 1900 and our ally in 1914. His world stature was immense. In 1927 he had written a book whose purpose was to describe, in its many manifestations, the 'fundamental factor operative towards the making or creation of wholes in the universe.' If our world is really permeated by this universal factor, it must be of importance to know about it and — in so far as in us lies — to participate in it as well. Smuts was therefore offering a concept of almost unsurpassable importance. But we do all our intellectual communication, and nearly all our accurate thinking, in words. A concept therefore remains incommunicable and almost unthinkable unless we have an acceptable word in which it can be designated.

Through the Greek ὅλος = Whole, Jan Smuts allowed himself to 'coin' (as he said) the word 'Holism' for the factor which he was describing in his book.[6] It would be wrong to say that the word has never been used at all. It occurs several times in the Alpach Symposium created by sixteen of the most powerful thinkers in the western world.[7] But it has never taken root even in the conversations of tertiarily educated people. It was probably half strangled at birth by its illegitimate visual link with holiness. Be that as it may, in fourteen years in the Senior Common Room at St Luke's College, I never heard the word spoken once. For all practical purposes it is stone dead and nothing can bring it to life.

By a strange twist of misfortune, there is one area in which 'holism' is alive. Almost all educated people have heard of 'holistic medicine'. Actually holistic medicine is quite a good idea. It means that instead of trying to kill symptoms with chemicals, we should consider the whole patient in his or her whole environment. This is in fact practised, or at least seriously attempted, by many doctors and in many hospitals. But by the folly of its advocates or the cunning of its enemies, holistic medicine has come to mean anti-doctor and anti-hospital medicine. In this way, so far as it is not dead, 'Holism' is understood to mean 'Pottiness'.

My proposed spelling is not original. A few people, and at least one small organisation, already write the word in the more acceptable way; a recent useful book spells it correctly through the text and in the sub-title.[8] It is far more important that much larger numbers of people, and several significant organisations, are already heading in a wholist direction without actively using the word in either of its spellings. They may make better progress if they have an acceptable word for their common destination. They may be more effective if they know that they are not engaged on a task so unrewarding as the attempted

[6] *Holism and Evolution* (Macmillan, 1927) p. 100.

[7] Now published as *Beyond Reductionism*, Koestler and Smithies eds, (Hutchinson, 1969).

[8] *Breaking Through: Theory and Practice of Wholistic Living*, by Walter and Dorothy Schwarz (Green Books, 1987).

deployment of facts and arguments addressed to the intellects of unchanged people in the hope of persuading them to make revolutionary changes in the disastrous policies that are now being pursued. Their common task is to bring forth increasing numbers of people who have changed at those levels of their own being which are normally described as religious — changed, that is to say, in their deep understanding of their own nature and purpose as human beings, and of their relatedness to the whole of life past present and future, and to the ultimate reality which underlies the whole situation in which they live. If the supporters of forward-looking movements are tempted to quail — as many of them often are — when they see the huge financial and propaganda power of the institutions that fight against them; if they are daunted by the dead weight of inertia imposed by personal and social selfishness; then they may feel a new hope when they realise that perhaps the inestimable power of a living religion might be brought into play on what now seems to be the weaker side.

3

We Are Called to Advance

I have already referred to *The Significance of Jesus* which was written by W. R. Maltby in 1929.[1] Two particularly impressive sentences have dominated my thinking ever since I read them in the 1940s. In the 1970s I found that the same basic thought had been expressed in two sentences spoken by Wolfgang Pauli just a couple of years before Maltby was writing. Maltby was a well loved leader in the English Free Church; Pauli was an Austrian scientist and a member of the Einstein-Bohr-Heisenberg team. The sentences do not depend for their significance on the authors who wrote and spoke them. They are decisive because they seem to be true. Maltby, in the first of his two sentences wrote:

> There is, I believe, already within reach a nobler, more reasonable, more comprehensive message than ever our fathers knew — and this not because we are wiser, or even more sincere than they, but because it is not for nothing that the Spirit of God has been at work upon the minds of men during these years of amazing research and fearless interrogation.

Pauli was considering the best values available to any society at any particular time; and he said:

> But if he himself is to live by these values, the average man has to be convinced that the spiritual framework embraces the entire wisdom of his society.

[1] See p. 4 above.

Maltby's sentence can be turned round and abbreviated so as to tell us that our forefathers, not because they were stupider or less sincere than we, had to make do with a less noble, less reasonable, less comprehensive message than has now been put into our reach by our God-given scientific and critical abilities. Pauli's can be similarly reversed so as to warn us that the average man will not live by the best values of his day if the spiritual framework seems to embrace facts and concepts which he knows to be untrue.

Maltby's second sentence is sad; Pauli's can be seen retrospectively as charged with menace. Maltby:

> That better message, however, has not yet been so articulated as to reach the average man, and if he asks only where and how to begin, he may have to wait long before he hears any satisfying answer.

Pauli's words, though not published in English until 1971, are reported to have been spoken in 1927:

> In Western culture, for instance, we may well reach the point in the not too distant future where the parables and images of the old religion will have lost their persuasive force even for the average person; when that happens, I am afraid that all the old ethics will collapse like a house of cards and that unimaginable horrors will be perpetrated.[2]

In Pauli's part of Europe, the unimaginable horrors began about six years later; and I cannot exonerate the leaders of the Church from some share of responsibility for the collapse of the old ethics.

Some who made earlier attempts to reconcile science and religion — for example, the members of the Modern Churchman's Union in the early years of our century —

[2] Maltby in *The Significance of Jesus* (SCM, 1929) pp.39/40; Pauli quoted by Werner Heisenberg in *Physics and Beyond* (George Allen & Unwin, 1971) pp. 83–4.

were accused of gleefully lopping off essential parts of the Church's message so as to retreat from the traditional Truth itself. More traditional churchmen could regard themselves as the gallant defenders of the eternal citadel against the threat that was spreading from the 'evil' of our contemporary scientific and critical competence. Verses from the Old Testament encouraged these people to regard themselves as the faithful 'remnant' upholding the Truth of God amidst a population of earth-bound clods who were incapable of rising to the Church's glorious Truth. This seems to be almost the opposite of our actual situation. We are challenged, not to stand firm against a proposed retreat, but to make the changes that are now required by the God-given increase in our abilities. Jesus said: 'I have yet many things to say to you, but you cannot bear them now. Howbeit, when he, the Spirit of truth, is come he will guide you into all truth'.[3] This was not to be a once-for-all experience fully completed before the end of the first century. It is a steadily developing process embracing the whole human race in the past, through our present and into the future. To this process the Church has to respond, not by retreating, but by making the appropriate advance. The majority of our people live without any serious religion largely because the 'Message' which they hear from the Church is intellectually and spiritually below the level of the better message to which they might respond.

As we have seen, this necessity is bound to be superficially unwelcome to most of our bishops and to other prominent leaders in the Church because it will involve a short-term disturbance in their dwindling institution.[4] But we have reached the point of crisis. *Either* the institution will be disturbed; *or* the Church will persist on the path towards its slow death.

One thing seems quite certain. In no way can the leaders of the Church articulate the more reasonable message now

[3] John 16. 12–13.
[4] See p. 13 above.

within our reach except through openly repudiating parts of the less reasonable message that was accepted by so many of our ancestors in more ignorant days. In no way can they construct a spiritual framework which embraces the entire wisdom of our society without openly discarding significant parts of the framework which does not. I am therefore saying much more than that the Church's contemporary message will never win the contemporary people. In the next chapter we shall consider the fiendish pressures exerted by our deep self-centred emotions on our conscious minds. Because of these pressures, the message which we hear from the Church *actually is* the cause of our irreligious state.

Some people will feel that this suggestion is too outrageous to deserve a moment's serious consideration. But are they necessarily right? The answer may depend a good deal on how much of the Church's story we think we have heard and experienced already. If we feel that we have known most of it, then it will surely seem intolerable that anyone should suggest drastic change in what has been going on through all these hundreds and hundreds of years. But what if we have so far read no more than the early chapters of the story? Suppose, if only for the sake of argument, that we do not destroy all life on earth sometime in the next two hundred years. On this supposition, how will our present state appear to those who look back on it, say, from the middle of the fifth millennium AD? Dietrich Bonhoeffer may have been unwise when he said that 'man has come of age'. To dismiss his whole theme, the orthodox needed only to list the follies and wickedness of the people of our time. But what if the recent explosion in our knowledge and understanding has led humanity over the watershed between a relatively safe childhood and a bewildering and dangerous adolescence? If this, by analogy, is a fair description of our present state, teaching methods that worked quite well during our childhood may be positively disastrous in our early human adolescence.

Without doubt some of today's church-goers would be

deeply disturbed if leaders of the Church set out to offer the Truth in ways that might fit the state of our contemporary majority. These would be sincere and honourable people. It must be repeated that there is nothing morally wrong in those who can still accept the Truth in the ways in which majorities could accept it until fairly recent times. But two questions arise. Are we really confronted with an Eleventh Commandment: 'Thou shalt not upset a church-goer.'? The other question is about the percentage of church-goers who would be permanently disturbed. On the first page of the argument of his deeply erudite book Hans Küng asked: 'Are there not today in all Churches many people who do not want to remain at the childhood stage in their faith.'[5] I believe that there are, and that they may today form an outright majority of those who still attend church services. We have seen that the 'sharp pain' of the 1960s soon reverted to a 'dull ache'.[6] But even a dull ache is something from which most people would like to escape. Wouldn't it be exciting for most church-goers if their leaders offered them a message which would enable them to fight back against the irreligious ambience of our day with some hope of success? Wouldn't it be good if we could carry the traditional Truth, albeit in a necessarily new dress, to the exceptionally able and upright persons who have repudiated it at one time or another 'for honest and decent reasons'?[7]

The unavoidable disturbance in the institution does not necessarily mean that the Church has to split. It may be difficult, but in these days it ought not to be impossible, for institutions to be disturbed without splitting. It happened before in the thirteenth century! There was then 'one of the greatest revolutions in thinking about God that has ever occurred.' It did not happen without fierce argument between some churchmen and others; but there was no split in the institution. This was entirely unknown to me until Peter Hebblethwaite wrote an article for the

[5] *On being a Christian* (Collins, 1978) p. 19.
[6] See p. 8–9 above.
[7] See p. 11 above.

Guardian on Christmas Eve 1987. For sure, they failed to avoid the split in the 1500s: but, if they could change their ideas about God without splitting the Church in the 13th century, we ought to be able to do it again today.[8] Everything will depend on mutual charity across the lines of the disturbance. Those who see the need for fundamental change in the Church's way of offering the Truth must charitably acknowledge — as I have already acknowledged — the sincerity and personal moral value of those who still receive the message in much the same ways as those in which it was widely accepted in a not very distant past.[9] But these people, being a quite small percentage of our whole population, must charitably acknowledge the sincerity of an even smaller minority, namely those who know that a living religion is a basic requirement for social good health; who see that a living religion is no longer reaching the people from the Church; and who therefore understand that on any long view the top social priority, bar none, is to puzzle out the ways in which the unchanging Truth about life might be effectively carried to our ever-changing people.[10] Our integrity must be charitably respected even by those who are confident that our suggestions are mistaken.

After all, something must have gone wrong. The statistics of the Church look like the weight chart of a patient with anorexia from which one can almost forecast the date of death. They are set out in great detail, though for a single unnamed country diocese, in the appendices to *Rural Anglicanism.*[11] In less detail, but for the whole country, the figures were offered in the Preface to *Crock-*

[8] Readers who missed the article may have a copy by writing to *13th C: Reformation*, College, Broadclyst, Exeter enclosing SAE and (with apologies) a 13p stamp to meet cost of photocopying. I am indebted to the *Guardian* and to Peter Hebblewaite for permission to send these copies.

[9] See p. 12–13 above.

[10] See p. 15 above.

[11] By Leslie Francis (Collins, 1985) pp. 172–8

ford's Clerical Directory 1987/88.[12] The author believed, and those who agreed with him still believe, that everything is trending downwards *because* the leaders of the Church, whom they regard as 'compromisers', are giving away far too much to the liberal theologians of our day. Could the truth be opposite? Could the Church's 'calm and unobtrusive alienation in thought and spirit from the great silent multitude of Englishmen'[13] stem from the fact that religious leaders, to avoid any upset in their institution, are compromising far too much with some of our Evangelicals and High Anglicans? This must be considered more carefully in the next chapter. Meanwhile I can do no more than repeat my two convictions. Given mutual charity, the institution need not split. But *either* the institution will be disturbed; *or* the Truth will not reach the people.

Postscript

Some of the High Anglicans and Evangelicals say 'I stand on the Bible' as if that ends the argument. But should they so stand as to use the Bible like a weapon against modern knowledge? Or should we use modern knowledge to understand the Bible more deeply than ever before? No-one should either swallow the whole Bible uncritically, or dismiss it contemptuously, without having read *The Good Book* by Brian Redhead and Frances Gumley (Duckworth, 1987).

[12] 'Between 1960 and 1982 the rate of infant baptism for each 1000 of the population fell from 554 to 347. Easter communicants fell from 2,339,000 to 1,674,000, and the number of annual confirmations from 190,713 to 84,566. It would appear that fewer than 5 per cent of the English population could be regarded as Anglican churchgoers.' *Op: Cit: (Church House Publishing 1987), p.68.*

[13] See F.J.A. Hort quoted on p. vi above.

4

To Embrace The Entire Wisdom

I believe that Wolfgang Pauli was right. The vast majority of our contemporaries will persist in their religionless state until they are offered a spiritual framework which manifestly embraces all that is so clearly good and true in the new knowledge and understanding which have burst out and spilled over to ordinary men and women in the course of the last two centuries. It is time to look at this great body of wisdom to see how the teaching of the Church needs to be unambiguously changed as we move from our human childhood and into our human adolescence.

'Original Sin'

Contemporary leaders of the Church allow religion to suffer ignominious defeat when they wrap up one of the profoundest human truths in a discardable medieval phrase. They do this at a time when our collective ignorance is exposing the human race to greater dangers than confronted our ancestors at any earlier time; and when the truth could be firmly established by a not very profound study of the common findings of all conflicting schools of contemporary psychology. Persistence in language appropriate to our human childhood is preventing a more adolescent way of teaching from going onto the offensive against the real contemporary enemy of religion. This enemy of religion was described several decades ago by J.H. Oldham when he wrote:

> The most serious competitor of the Christian faith in the world today is what we can describe as salvation

> through knowledge. That is the working religion of men everywhere, the driving force of the modern world. It is what makes the wheels go round alike in capitalist America, in western Europe, in the Communist East and in the fermenting continents of Asia and Africa.[1]

Oldham was describing the so-called 'Religion of Science' defined by Beatrice Webb as 'the implicit faith that by the methods of physical science, and by these methods alone, could be solved all the problems arising out of the relations of man to man and of man towards the universe.'[2]

The supreme manifestation of this faith burst on the academic world in 1936 in *Language, Truth and Logic* by A.J. (later Professor Sir Alfred) Ayer. His Logical Positivism was founded on the assertion that no statement can be significant unless he who makes it can tell us the evidence by which it could be sustained if true, or overturned if false. There can be no doubt that the evidence — often described as 'repeatable and publicly testable evidence' — had to come from intellectually established facts supported by intellectually unchallengeable argument. It was all made to sound very plausible, and the whole academic world lapped it up. I am surprised that our universities seemed so untroubled by the fact that those who accepted Ayer's methodology, *by that very acceptance*, dismissed religion in all its possible forms and rejected any attempt to find meaning or purpose in human life; and this because any statement about either of these is immediately reduced to insignificance by Logical Positivism or by any of its variants.

I have been told that Professor Ayer rejected his own thesis some time in the 1970s; but far more recently than that, in a television challenge to Donald Cupitt, I heard him hammering his key argument: 'Where is your *evidence?*' On top of that, no recent change in Ayer's

[1] *Life is Commitment* (SCM, 1953) pp. 18/19.
[2] *My Apprenticeship* (Longmans, 1926) p.83.

outlook can alter the fact that our social life is now dominated by men and women who formed their basic assumptions in decades when our universities were saturated in this cult of irreligious meaninglessness. Professors and lecturers must not excuse themselves from responsibility by saying that they did not teach in any Department of Philosophy — not unless they can point to some public and unambiguous protest against Ayer's faith. Such self-exculpation would fly in the face of a little known but basic law of communication. *Silence is never neutral*! Silence is always the loudest way of supporting what is going on all around. People must take responsibility for their silences as well as for their words.

The outcome of this almost unanimous tertiary education has been proclaimed by Viktor Frankl, the psychiatrist who survived Buchenwald. He described 'more and more patients complaining of an inner emptiness, a sense of total and ultimate meaninglessness of their lives'; and he set up, as the basic emotional force in man, '*the will to meaning* in contrast to the Adlerians' will to power and the Freudians' will to pleasure.'[3] Of the aimlessness of people's lives, C.G. Jung wrote: 'I should not object if this were called the general neurosis of our age.'[4] Professor Waddington said: 'Our present society is actively repressing the search for meaning.'[5] In short, the universities of our century have been actively propagating the general neurosis of our century. Small wonder if we are now a psychologically sick society.

A minor point interests me. Why did not the leaders of the Church use their privileged access to the mass media so as to launch a public attack on the Logical Positivists? They seemed to think it enough if they persisted with the continuing assertion of their 'Message' without noticing what other people were doing to the audience that needed to know the Truth. Semi-consciously they may have known that a public attack on Professor Ayer would publicise his

[3, 5] *Beyond Reductionism* pp. 399–400 & 418; italics original.

[4] Quoted from *Archetype*, by Anthony Stevens (Routledge & Kegan Paul, 1982) p.30.

counter attack which would have been devastating. In this situation it probably seemed better to say nothing in the hope that relatively few church-goers would ever hear of Logical Positivism. This is what actually happened, so perhaps the shrewd policy was justified. But in most colleges and universities it left the students defenceless against men like Professor O'Connor.[6]

Even when 'Original' is left out of the formula, there is a widespread misunderstanding of Sin. It is taken to refer to something that someone has done quite consciously in spite of clearly knowing that it was morally wrong. It happens; and it does not need to be spelled out with particular examples. But most of us, if asked whether we had culpably yielded to a known temptation during the last seven days, would say in all sincerity that we had not. Hence the frequent final stage in the rejection of religion with: 'Anyway, I'm not a miserable sinner.' This is shallow self-confidence. In fact, belief in the omni-competence of human intellect is contrary not only to Christianity, but to all the great religious traditions of the world. As he worked towards his conclusion in *Varieties of Religious Experience*, William James wrote that 'the warring gods and formulas of the various religions do indeed cancel each other, but there is a certain uniform deliverance in which religions all appear to meet.' It consists, he said, of two parts of which the first is 'a sense that there is *something wrong about us*, as we naturally stand.'[7] For our ignorance of this basic truth I must blame not only the Church, but also the whole company of our psychologists and all our intellectuals.

Provided that anyone is emotionally motivated so that

[6] See pp. 7–8 above.

[7] *Op. cit:* (Longmans Green & Co, 1901) p. 508; or (Fount, 1977) p. 484; italics original. The second part of the common deliverance will be considered in a later chapter.

he can receive it, the truth can be found in a not very deep reading of our century's psychological writings. Yet neither the whole company of the psychologists, nor any outstanding psychologist, has ever proclaimed it so as to make it unmistakeably clear to all reasonably educated people. And no intellectual has dug into the psychologists' erudite writings so as to bring out their basic simple truth because, had he done so, he would have discredited the Religion of Science. The fact is, however, that *intellect is unreliable when facing problems that involve personal or group self-interest*. By parody on William James one can say that the warring words and formulas of various psychologies may indeed cancel each other, but there is a certain uniform deliverance in which psychologists all appear to meet. Emotional complexes are built into our depths by inheritance from our parents and by our experiences in the environment where we live. Some psychologists say that the inheritance is not only from father and mother; on the contrary, deep archetypal predispositions are built into us from an array of ancestors reaching back into pre-history. This seems to me to be true; but however it may be, we are wholly or largely unaware of our emotional complexes which are outside the control of anything so feeble as intellect. In one way or another these emotional complexes are almost invariably self-centred. Far from conscious thoughts determining the way we feel, it is more nearly true to say that our feelings determine the way we think. This happens through the process known as *rationalisation* by which the deep complexes filter into our conscious minds the facts and arguments which support what they want us to think and believe and do; and filter the other facts and arguments out. It is for this reason that intellect is unreliable when facing questions which emotionally involve our personal or group self-interest; and for this reason that there is 'something wrong about us as we naturally stand.' Our intellectuals remain ignorant of this truth of human nature despite the facts and arguments being available to them in the psychologists' writings. They remain ignorant because they are emotionally conditioned to keep the relevant facts and arguments out of their conscious minds.

This ignorance need not endure. If leaders of the Church dropped their medieval phraseology and seriously tried to teach the truth in contemporary ways, we could quite soon shatter the Religion of Science and establish a large company of men and women and adolescents who would be less cocksure about their own opinions and more watchful for the possibility that their intellectual judgments had been palmed off on them, through rationalisations, by the subconscious emotional forces in the depths. Some years ago I found no difficulty in conveying these truths to a group of adolescents who had been selected for a week's holiday on the Isle of Iona because of their coming from disturbed homes in Glasgow.[8]

If the real human truth were more widely known, the Church would make changes in the wording of our confessions. Until quite recently congregations said of their sins that 'the remembrance of them is grievous unto us, the burden of them is intolerable.' For most of those present, this was simply untrue. Even now, in the most recent Alternative Service Book, our attention is directed to what we have done and left undone which, presumably, we are supposed to know about. But that is just the point. Perhaps one church-goer in every hundred, on any Sunday, has been so struck by Reality during the last seven days as to recognise some almost unforgiveable act of personal selfishness. But because of rationalisation, the rest, in all conscious sincerity, believe that they have been pretty well all right. If we gather for confession — and it seems a valuable thing to do — we should be mainly remembering, and sympathising with each other as we remember, not what we have consciously done, but what we inevitably are. We are creatures capable of profound selfishness *while consciously believing ourselves righteous*. And then, recalling the Parable of the Prodigal Son, we

[8] See *We Teach Them Wrong* (Gollancz, 1963) Chapter 9. I might put the argument rather differently today; but it was written from experience.

can rejoice together because, if we do not hypocritically pretend to be better than we are, we can be accepted despite all our defects.

Our almost inevitable rejection of the truth when offered in the Church's outdated way, and our consequent belief in our own intellectual omni-competence, impose on us a situation which is truly appalling. In our present state of ignorance we too easily divide people into 'Me-and-Those-who-Agree-with-Me' who are certainly and obviously right: and 'Those-Others' who are just as surely wrong. Because of our ignorance we assert total righteousness for ourselves; and then, through the psychological process known as *projection*, we impute total evil to the others. This inflames every human disagreement from family quarrels, through arguments on trivial or vital committees, through industrial disputes and finally reaching to the mutual suspicions which rage between the two most powerful nations on earth.

'But *I* say "*Love* your enemies" '.[9] It is appallingly difficult to do it. But at least we might respect our enemies if we knew that we and they share the same human disability; and that their emotional state and the whole of their past history led them to their sincere opinions, just as our emotional state and history have led us to ours. P.W. Martin, whom I have already mentioned[10] , explained the real human truth which is so sadly disguised in the Church's medieval phraseology, and then wrote:

> That the world is governed by men who do not now know about Original Sin is far more dangerous than that it was once governed by men who did not know that bubonic plague is carried by rats.

Martin was writing in *Learning for Teaching*, but I have to quote from memory. As with Maltby and Pauli, the importance of the words depends, not on the author, but

[9] Matthew 5.44.
[10] See p. 10 above.

on their truth. We shall see at a later stage that our ignorance of Original Sin, when its reality is understood in the light of contemporary psychology, not only enhances the danger of our destroying all life in nuclear war. It also makes it impossible for any except small minorities to know that we ought to be making common sacrifices now so as to prepare for the not very distant day when our children and grandchildren will have to live on the planet's annual income. E.H. Carr's devastating judgment deserves to be considered in relation to this challenge.[11]

If the truth that is hidden in a discardable phrase can now be taught through contemporary psychology, what could the leaders of the Church learn from it themselves? This is one of the most important issues raised anywhere in the book, and I am anxious to handle it carefully. To be fair to the bishops and to other leaders in the Church, it must be affirmed that most of them are not Fundamentalists. But they seem to believe that there is some way — that there simply must be some way — in which, on the one hand, they can proclaim the Truth in ways that ought to be acceptable to the huge majority of our religionless contemporaries while, on the other hand, they offer warm and unruffled support to the dwindling minorities who can still accept the Truth as it was accepted by majorities in our fairly recent past.

As a relatively small item, leaders of the Church should ask whether they themselves are being influenced by 'Original Sin' as this old phrase can now be understood. Are their own deep semi-conscious emotional preferences filtering into their conscious minds the facts and arguments which suggest that both parts of their double act can be simultaneously sustained, while filtering the other facts and arguments out?

Far more important conclusions could be reached if bishops would look carefully at the religionless majority in the light of all that is now displayed by the psychologists. The central truth, as the bishops themselves would gladly

[11] See p. 4 above.

proclaim it, is that humans are born as self-centred creatures. The same truth can be asserted by saying that a majority of our contemporaries *do not want to be religious in any serious way*. Of course, any genuine religious belief leads on to increased inner unity, more purposeful living and peace in a distracted world. But the first steps in such a religious direction will call for some kinds of serious effort at times which could otherwise be given to immediate pleasures. Anyone who spends even five minutes seriously wondering whether religion may deserve some kind of consideration, has taken a tiny step away from self and towards the possibility of something greater. It has already been pointed out that the emotional forces in the depths are almost bound to be self-centred. These forces therefore do their best to prevent people from taking the first steps in a religious direction. Such forces 'know' that they would fail if they put the matter directly. Few could respect themselves if they had to say 'I am irreligious because I am a self-centred hedonistic sloven.' The deep forces have to put up better arguments — more plausible rationalisations — if they are to win. These rationalisations are handed out to them if a religious attitude to life can seem to be associated with a whole array of picturesque accretions which are no longer acceptable. Momentarily someone turns in a religious direction. Immediately the deep self-centred forces throw up such thoughts as that religion means all those animals getting into a big boat; a star actually appearing to stand still in the sky; the world made by a Big Invisible Man; a baby born without sex between the parents. Struck by such ideas as these, people can all too readily suppose that they are being intelligent and up-to-date, rather than self-centred, when they turn back from those first steps in a religious direction. They can retain their irreligion and their self-respect both at the same time. This is what the deep self-centred forces wanted them to do. The leaders of the Church do not seem to be considering the situation as deeply as they should.

The problem is particularly acute in most of our universities. If a university has some 5,000 students, there could be up to 250 members of the Universities' and Colleges' Christian Fellowship.[12] They are passionate evangelisers. In the first three weeks of each autumn term at least nine tenths of the first-year students will be personally challenged with the Fundamentalists' message and with 'Are you saved?' By the end of the year the evangelisers may rejoice in 100 converts. This will leave about 4,500 students who have been 'told' that Christianity means believing in a whole array of propositions which lie outside — and are indeed flatly contrary to — the huge outburst of knowledge and understanding which has been given to the human race in the last two hundred years. Subjectively the members of UCCF fight the good fight with all their might. Objectively they spread amongst our most alert and intelligent people all the rationalisations they need for dismissing religion as something irrelevant to the late twentieth century.

The failure to understand the problem is displayed when church-goers turn on me almost angrily to say that hardly any bishop would today insist that religion depends on our accepting Noah's Ark, the star standing still, the Big Invisible Man or even (perhaps) the Virgin Birth. This raises a difficult point. It may well be that most bishops do not now insist that religion *does* require us to believe all that was so easily believed two or three hundred years ago. The question is whether bishops have publicly proclaimed that it does *not*. A basic law of communication must be recalled. *Silence is never neutral!* Silence is the loudest way of supporting what is going on all around. And what is it that goes on around our bishops? I have several times been told that my whole argument must be wrong simply because the best filled churches are those where the Fundamentalists' message is most resolutely proclaimed in all its purity. But of course! I am not making any personal attack on any group of church-goers. There is nothing to condemn if some five per cent of our people can still accept

[12] This is the relatively new name for what was long known as the Inter-Varsity Fellowship.

religious truth in the same way as majorities accepted it in earlier days. But five per cent of the population of such a city as Exeter comes to more than five thousand people — quite enough to fill three or four churches with enthusiastic congregations. This fact, far from casting doubt on my argument, positively sustains it. Precisely because these are the best filled churches and the most enthusiastic congregations, it is the easiest thing in the world for the huge religionless majority to look at them, to know — or at least to know dimly — what message they offer and receive, and then to say to themselves: 'So *that's* religion, is it? Thank you very much. It's not for me.' Thus the silence of the bishops in face of the minorities who are still sincere Fundamentalists — that is to say one half of the double act in which they hope to succeed — is actually doing 'the Devil's' work for him. It disguises from people the fact that they are being hedonistic and self-centred, and allows them to believe that they are being scientific, when they close their minds against religion in any possible form. It encourages them to ignore the possibility that they, and their whole community, may be in danger of perishing for want of a living religion which embraces the entire wisdom of our society. The assertions appropriate to humanity's religious childhood, and still acceptable to sincere but dwindling minorities, are heard by those who now constitute the potentially more adolescent spiritual majority. In their minds they serve as 'rationalisation fodder' enabling them to close themselves against religious possibilities while retaining their self respect.

I must charitably try to recognise the possibility that my conclusions may be wrong. But, in my own mind, the last three paragraphs have established the point so tersely offered at the end of the previous chapter. The Church is dying because its leaders compromise too much, not with the liberal theologians of today, but with some of the traditionalists who know the Truth — sincerely and deeply know the Truth — in ways that were acceptable to the majority not very long ago. We must now consider other aspects of the common wisdom of our contemporary society which require unambiguous assertion by the leaders of the Church if the Truth is to reach the people.

Miracles

In relatively recent times, the physical miracles have changed sides. Not very long ago people perceived prophetic or even divine qualities in those who could do such mighty works as our holy books report. Today at least nine tenths of the top formers in our secondary schools and of students in our colleges ask why they should pay attention to books containing so many stories which are obviously impossible. Teachers today have to show that our Gospels deserve attention, not because of the miracle stories, but in spite of them. If the work is tackled courageously, there is no serious difficulty. It begins by clearly describing the Gospel-making process.

Everything known about Jesus was carried for the first few decades on oral tradition — that is to say on the mouth-to-ear-to-mouth enthusiasm of the earlier followers as they talked with those who came later. Today we do not guess or suppose, *we know*, that this process has invariably resulted in the emergence of wonder tales around any great religious leader. Some of these tales were included, in all good faith, in the earliest written records. In the conditions of the first century it would have been impossible for the news about Jesus to be told and retold for twenty years or more, and then to be written down, without its gathering around itself the accounts of such miracles as we can read today. But is there nothing else in our Gospels? In our century, as well as knowing that wonder tales inevitably collected around religious leaders, we also know that insight — by far the most precious possession of humanity — is never invented in the excited babbling of excited followers. If there is insight in the Gospels, it points to one who was its source. This knowledge does not impose on us the sad necessity of religious retreat which the faithful must resist to the bitter end. It enables us to make a religious advance and to read the

Gospels at a depth which was not possible until recently. At every point we can ask: is this genuine insight; or is it the kind of thing that could have been invented, or the sort of gloss that could have been imposed, by the early converts in the first century? In this light we can look at the story of the temptations. (1) Turn stones into bread. Jesus refused to tackle economic problems. (2) Jump off the Temple. Jesus refused to win by wonders. (3) Bow down and worship *me*. Jesus refused to use force[13]. Because of our recently acquired critical abilities, we can now see that these are the courses which would have been considered and rejected by one who felt called to a unique mission. But these abilities were not available to the men and women of the first century. Excited followers could never have invented what we can now read. The story of the temptation is in our record because Jesus described his rejected courses to his first followers in easily remembered allegories.

It was the most natural thing in the world for the early enthusiasts to say and sincerely to believe, for example, that Jesus walked on the water. For several centuries — as I see it through the whole childhood of the Church — Christians read the story and marvelled at the divine power of one who could work such a miracle. But what in the early days of our human adolescence? Sixth formers know that when any body — including a human body — is placed, or places itself, on the surface of a liquid, it will sink in until it has displaced a volume of liquid whose weight is equal to the weight of the body. This, of course, is Archimedes' Theorem; and sixth formers know that it works, not a billion times out of a billion and one, but every single time without any exception ever. If the message which they hear from the Church seems to be inviting them to choose either religion or Archimedes, the great majority will choose Archimedes. That is what 'the Devil' would want them to do.

The educational aspect of our new understanding is less

[13] Matthew 4. 1–11.

important than the religious. It was natural for early Christians to say that Jesus walked on the water. We know that he who rejected the second temptation would never have belittled himself by actually doing it. The whole of this argument is upheld by *Doctrine in the Church of England* which was published as long ago as in 1938 by an authoritative Commission under the chairmanship of William Temple while he was Archbishop of York. It is perhaps the most important secret religious document of the twentieth century. 'It has to be recognised', wrote the authors, that:

> legends involving abnormal events have tended to grow very easily in regard to great religious leaders, and that in consequence it is impossible in the present state of knowledge to make the same evidential use of the narratives of miracles in the Gospels which appeared possible in the past.

Even today some of our religious teachers and preachers would read these words with sadness. 'Oh, dear'! We can't now make converts as they used to do in the past.' Temple and his colleagues took the opposite view. 'This is a religious gain', they wrote, 'inasmuch as the use of miracles to force belief appears to have been deliberately rejected by our Lord.'[14]

My ordained friends often try to dodge the impact of the expanded wisdom of our society by saying that the argument is irrelevant because the miracle stories contain spiritual or symbolic truth. Of course they do! I would not timidly admit, but would firmly proclaim, this important fact. It is important because mythological or allegorical stories often carry real power into our depths more surely than can intellectual argument based on ascertained facts. This is true, for example, of walking on the water. As the disciples wrestled with the sudden storm, they were upheld, like millions of people from that day to this, by their experience of the strength and nearness of Jesus. But

[14] *Op. cit:* (SPCK, 1938) p. 51.

the overwhelming majority of our contemporaries are not open to spiritual or symbolic meaning if it is offered to them on behalf of an institution which seems to be asking them to half-believe in factual truth as well. Christian teachers need to be unambiguous about the historical facts before our people will be open to the spiritual significance.

Virgin Birth and Resurrection

In the Christian tradition, the Virgin Birth and the Resurrection have been more important than all the other miracles put together, and the Bishop of Durham expressed his views about both of these in 1985. Nearly half a century earlier, William Temple and his fellow Commissioners set out the traditional belief in the Virgin Birth and then continued:

> There are some amongst us who hold that a full belief in the historic Incarnation is more consistent with the supposition that our Lord's birth took place under the normal conditions of human generation.

It is true that protests from traditionalists in 1938–39 prevented Temple's Report from ever being officially endorsed by the Church Assembly. But the authors included men who were, or who subsequently became, Archbishop of Canterbury, Bishops of Ripon, Derby, Chelmsford, Nottingham and Glasgow, Deans of St Paul's and Winchester, Vice-Chancellors of Cambridge and Manchester Universities and Regius Professor of Divinity at Oxford. These men unanimously agreed that both views of the Virgin Birth 'are held by members of the Church, as of the Commission, who fully accept the reality of our Lord's Incarnation.'[15] Why, then, did neither of our Archbishops publicly rebuke the vociferous company of Evangelicals and High Anglicans who would not have allowed us, in Durham, even one bishop who publicly took the

[15] *Op. cit:* pp. 82–3.

second of the two views which had been so long ago, and so weightily, declared to be acceptable in the English Church?

For sure the Bishop of Durham caused more outrage by his words on the Resurrection than by those on the Virgin Birth; and I must mildly reprove him for giving the mass media their chance with his hurtful phrase about 'a conjuring trick with bones.' Using many more words, the same point could have been made by asking whether our belief in the Resurrection depends on our asserting such an exact molecule-by-molecule reconstruction of the physical body of Jesus as would have made it visible even to the eye of Caiaphas if the High Priest had been peeping through a hole in the wall of the upper room. Through nineteen hundred years — through what I count as the childhood of the Christian Church — far more than nine tenths of church-going Christians would have answered the question with a confident affirmative. But is it the obligatory answer in the early stages of our human adolescence?

The decisive event must be the conversion of Paul described in the Acts of the Apostles.[16] This was real history. It actually happened; and its consequences were far-reaching. But there was no physical body present because we are told that Paul's companions saw no man; and they *would* have seen a physical body if it had been there. In his first letter to the Corinthians, Paul claimed exact identity between the experience given to him and the earlier experiences given to the other disciples.[17] Once again, the authors of *Doctrine in the Church of England* seem to embrace Dr Jenkins' views within the ambience of the Anglican faith. They wrote:

> When we ask 'What was it exactly that happened?' a variety of answers is possible. Belief that the Lord was risen is compatible both with a realisation that we cannot

[16] Acts 9. 1–7
[17] 1 Corinthians 15.8.

> expect to reach clear and full knowledge in detail, and also with a variety of critical views.[18]

William Temple, in his personal Introduction to the Report, proclaimed his own acceptance of the traditional view of both the decisive events. But he added:

> I fully recognise the position of those who sincerely affirm the reality of our Lord's Incarnation without accepting one or both of these two events as actual historical occurrences, regarding the records rather as parables than as history, a presentation of spiritual truth in narrative form.[19]

All this seems to be relevant in our days when so many are turned away from Christianity and — more important in my view — turned away from any openness to religion in any form, because they cannot accept the fact of the Virgin Birth or of the molecule-by-molecule reconstruction of a human body after its physical death.

If I wrote no more about the Bishop of Durham, I should be perpetuating the inevitable distortion imposed on him by the mass media. Questions about the Virgin Birth or the physical Resurrection can be offered in a very few attention-grabbing TV seconds or newspaper column inches; serious discussion of the meaning of the word 'God' would need much more time and space. So we have the public impression of a Bishop who would alarm the faithful at two particular points and leave the rest of the Church's message much as it is today. The Bishop's purpose is far greater. It is worth quoting significant parts of his address to the General Synod of the Church of England on July 6th 1986 so as to correct the imbalance of the media: in part, he said:

> The question is this. 'Is our God worth believing in?':

[18] *Op. cit* p. 84.
[19] *Op. cit:* p. 12.

> What sort of God are we portraying and believing in if we insist on what I will nickname 'the divine laser-beam' type of miracle as the heart and basis of the Incarnation and the Resurrection? I feel obliged to suggest to you, sisters and brothers in Christ, that if we do so insist then we are implying, if not actually portraying, a God who is, at the best, a cultic idol and, at the worst, the very devil. Let me try to explain this deeply troubling possibility . . . The choice of physical miracles with what might be called laser-beam precision and power, would not seem to be a choice that God cared, or would care, to use. For if such a physical transformation with precision and power is an option open to God consistent with his purposes of creation, freedom and love, then we are faced with a very terrible dilemma indeed. We are faced with the claim that God is prepared to work knock-down physical miracles in order to let a select number of people into the secret of his incarnation, resurrection and salvation but he is not prepared to use such methods in order to deliver from Auschwitz, prevent Hiroshima, overcome famine or bring about a bloodless transformation of apartheid. Such a God is surely a cultic idol . . . If such a God is not a cultic idol produced by mistaken and confused worshippers, but actually exists, then he must be the very devil. For he prefers a few selected worshippers to all the sufferers of our world. Such a god is certainly not worth believing in. But I do not believe that we can have possibly so learned Christ.

It was reported in several newspapers that about half of the members of the General Synod — normally regarded as a very conservative body — gave the Bishop a standing ovation. This leaves the other half sitting on their seats and we can suppose that some of these kept their hands by their sides. This confirms my view that the institution will have to be disturbed. But it allows the possibility that it need not be split, and the hope that many of its members will play a leading public part in the disturbing Reformation that is now needed.

What and Where is God?

Many preachers avoid any open reference to the questions raised by the Bishop of Durham by talking to us as if we all know what the word 'God' means. But we don't. We are descended from a host of ancestors who were allowed to conceptualise 'God' as referring to a Big Invisible Man. The saints and prophets and mystics always knew better, but they allowed the popular conceptualisation because they rightly felt that in those days it lifted the people a little nearer to the truth than they could otherwise come. Suddenly the situation is reversed. The Big Invisible Man, far from helping us towards the truth, now drives most of us away from it. This is bound to be painful for the dwindling minority who are still quite happy with the old understanding. But a change in our conceptualisation cannot be other than a religious advance. For the first time in Christian history, a majority of people know that the ultimate truth about life cannot be a supernatural Being 'out there'. By blithely talking about 'God' as if the word is to have the same meaning for us as it had for our great grandparents, the leaders of the Church belittle us by offering less than we are now capable of understanding. As a result, a ten-year-old boy confidently told me that he was irreligious because he did not believe that the world was made by God. He meant that he didn't believe it was made by a Big Invisible Man. He was right. It wasn't.

I have said already that those who were born after 1945 will hardly know about the spiritual explosion caused by *Honest to God.*[20] For a year or so, it seemed that John Robinson's paperback might trigger a genuine Reformation. At the heart of the controversy — specifically applauded by many of the enthusiasts, and flatly condemned by almost all the hostile critics — was a long

[20] See p. 8 above.

quotation from *The Shaking of the Foundations* where, in its two vital sentences, Paul Tillich had written of the word 'God':

> If that word has not much meaning for you, translate it, and speak of the depths of your life, of the source of your being, of your ultimate concern, of what you take seriously without any reservation. Perhaps, in order to do so, you must forget everything traditional that you have learned about God, perhaps even that word itself.[21]

Michael Ramsey, then the Archbishop of Canterbury, responded to the turmoil with commendable speed. In a matter of days rather than weeks he wrote a pamphlet, *Image Old and New*, in which he quoted the whole passage around which the controversy was raging, and then added:

> I think that quotation has meaning for us. It is an attempt to help a man who is estranged from ordinary religious talk but may find God by forgetting all ordinary religious talk, and thinking in depth about himself and his own meaning.

The weight and purport of the Archbishop's judgment can be underestimated by anyone who is misled by the words 'to help *a man*'. This can leave the impression that there may be, here and there, a minority of people who are estranged from ordinary religious talk; and that it was therefore rather considerate of the Bishop of Woolwich to offer suggestions which might be helpful to so small a company. In fact, 'estranged-from-ordinary-religious-talk' now describes about nine tenths of our contemporaries, and to this majority the Church should now be directing its ultimate concern.

It has to be added that the Archbishop went much further than to give subsequent approval to what Robinson

[21] *Op. cit:* (Pelican, 1962) p. 63; quoted by Robinson, *Op. cit:* (SCM, 1963) p.22.

was saying through his quotation from Tillich. He claimed that he himself had made the very same point three years earlier when he led a mission to Oxford. He quoted the first sentences from his opening address:

> I am going to be speaking about God. You would expect that. But I am not at the outset going to use the word 'God'. This is because the word has become conventional, and I am asking you to think about a reality rather than a word. It is also because I want to suggest that I am talking about what is already going on inside you, and not about a sort of outside technicality which I have come to sell to you.[22]

We therefore have the highest possible authority for the propriety of using translations for the word 'God'. There are plenty of other possibilities as well as those offered by Tillich. If it helps us we may think and speak of Ultimate Reality, deepest truth, Creator Spirit, meaning and purpose in life; we can use the Israeli 'I am', the Hindu 'Thou art That', the 'Logos' from the first line in St John's Gospel, or a phrase beloved by Einstein — the central order of things and events. I am uncertain about the propriety of using capital letters; here and elsewhere I sometimes use them and sometimes do not.

It is too little for a religious teacher to say that he never positively insists that people shall perceive God as a Big Invisible Man. Through racial memory we are now conditioned to respond to the word 'God' as our ancestors used to do. Having thus responded, most of us reject not only the old conception but the whole possibility of there being any religious dimension to life. Religious teachers must positively go into battle against the Big Invisible Man, and must repeatedly tell people to treat the word 'God' as a shorthand invitation to take up whichever translation has most meaning for them. Like all the other

[22] *Op. cit:* (SPCK, 1963) pp. 4–5, quoting from his *Introducing the Christian Faith* (SCM, 1960) p. 13.

suggestions in this chapter, the necessary change will mark a great religious advance.

Then where should we first look for God, or for ultimate reality, Deepest Truth or whatever translation anyone may prefer? Pagans, when uninstructed, could hardly prevent themselves from peopling their world with all kinds of godlings and spirits, all perfectly real and living outside themselves. When they were persuaded to see these as aspects of the one God, then He was naturally outside too. Until quite recently many good church-going people must have lived with this transcendent God 'out there' while only seldom making any contact with the same Reality which is immanent within. This situation, too, is quite suddenly reversed. The typical people of today will feel the Inner Truth, the vital spark in themselves, the creative link in their personal relationships, far more readily than they will recognise the transcendent God. It is a basic rule of teaching to start where the learners are; to offer first what comes easiest; and to hope that some of the learners will go on later to what is more difficult. The leaders of the Church seem now to be breaking this basic rule. The 'Message', as it would be heard in Songs of Praise from the BBC or in almost any church service, invites us to attend first of all to the transcendent God. This seems to be wrong because, when there has been a change on this scale in the spiritual outlook of the people, it is unreasonable for a great teaching institution to expect the people to change back so that it may persist in its old teaching ways. Even if it proves painful to those who have not yet followed the general trend, the teachers ought surely to change their ways of teaching so as to make contact with the majority of our people.

It will be seen that Archbishop Ramsey, when commenting on Robinson's book and when quoting from his own earlier words, approved not only of our using translations for the word 'God', but also of our directing our attention first to the immanent Truth. For this reason, in the next chapter, a suggested basic religious affirmation for our secular age will not first direct our attention to 'a sort of outside technicality which I have come to sell you'. For sure it will leave the way open and may even point in the direction of the transcendent Truth. But the first concern will be to consider 'what is already going on inside you' and to decide what sort of creatures human beings really are so that each may make his or her judgment about what he or she may really be in the depths. If the last two paragraphs have seemed reasonable, *The True Wilderness* by Harry Williams and *The Go-Between God* by John Taylor could be valuable reading.[23] I find these books very encouraging because Williams became Dean of Trinity in Cambridge and Taylor became Bishop of Winchester; and they show that a more contemporary style of teaching is already at work in the Church. I commend Taylor's book despite his making what I regard as the unwise suggestion that we should continue to speak of Original Sin and Fall of Man because, in earlier days, the phrases carried important spiritual truth.

The Impact of Evolution

Evolution is not a new item of information which simply adds itself to people's existing stock of knowledge. For sure, amongst our church-going minorities, there are a good many who have accepted the fact of evolution without its having changed them in their depths. But for most of us, awareness of evolution has transformed our whole outlook so that our religious understanding can never be the same as that of our quite recent ancestors who did not know that life on earth has evolved. Our feeling of relationship to past present and future is wholly transformed. I know that my friend and mentor, Canon Charles Raven, was thinking very largely of evolution when he wrote:

There have been in human history no developments in

[23] The books are published by Constable (1965) and SCM (1972), respectively.

> man's general outlook and habits so vast as those of the past century; it is unthinkable that they should not bring with them a development equivalently vast in the life and thought of the Church.[24]

His words were written well over half a century ago; and since then, far from his forecast being fulfilled, his 'unthinkable' has become the actual. There has been no development equivalently vast in the message that reaches the people from the Church.

How easy it must have been in the days of Archdeacon William Paley who wrote a book to show that man and nature could not be so wonderful as they are if God did not exist so as to have planned it all from the start. I was delighted when I read his adoration of the epiglottis:

> Reflect how frequently we swallow, how constantly we breathe. At a city feast, for example, what deglutition, what anhelation! Yet does this little cartilage so faithfully interpose its office, so securely guard the entrance to the windpipe, whilst morsel after morsel, draught after draught are coursing over it (which nevertheless must be open for breath every second of time) that not two guests are choked in a century.[25]

It is quite difficult for us to wipe out of mind our knowledge of evolution so as imaginatively to think ourselves back into the state of those who made Paley's book a best seller. 'Not because they were stupider than we.'[26] it must have been quite hard for them to look at the world all around, firmly to believe that it had been created in exactly the marvellous state in which they saw it, and then to reject the idea that it had been brought into existence by the Divine Planner.

[24] *A Wanderer's Way* (Martin Hopkinson, 1929) p.167.
[25] *Natural Theology* (S. Hamilton, 1813), quoted in *Evolutionary Theory and Christian Ethics* by David Lack (Methuen, 1957), p.61.
[26] See p. 33 above.

We know that life on earth has evolved from simplest beginning through millions and millions of years.

New discussions amongst scientists have brought us such headlines as 'Darwinism is Dead!' These can be legitimate if we go on to read no more than that there are now scientists who seriously question whether the simplest methods, proposed by the earliest Darwinians, can fully explain everything that has happened. John Peacocke, a physical biochemist and an Anglican priest, says quite rightly that:

> Confidence in the centrality of the neo-Darwinian explanation of the evolutionary process in principle is entirely consistent with acknowledging ignorance about how particular transformations came about in the inaccessible past.[27]

Christian propagandists behave childishly if they think they can win the modern world by challenging the scientists with: 'Ha! *Here* we have a development which your lot can't yet explain.' This takes us back to the 'God of the Gaps' — the Big Invisible Engineer at his celestial drawing board working out a 'divine laser-beam' to get things from A to B. It overemphasises the transcendent aspect of the Truth which came to people so naturally during the childhood of the Church. If it were now to be the great argument for God it would leave us with the transcendent Power, proved and present in the gaps, and unproved and probably absent everywhere else. In our human adolescence, we turn to a Creator Spirit who is at every moment immanent in the process which started before ever our planet was made, has led us to where we are, and points us to a future which, for good or ill, now depends in part on the decisions which we choose to take.

It is correct to say that some of our scientists are today finding that the whole process has been more mysterious

[27] *God and the New Biology* (J.M. Dent & Sons, 1986) p.39.

than Darwin and his early followers supposed. But scientists who express genuine uncertainty about the *methods* of evolution do not cast any doubt on the *fact* of evolution. No scientist worthy of the name will now deny that life started in the simplest unicellular creatures and has evolved through millions of years into what we see around us now. This remains true even when scientists know that they do not know exactly *how* it all happened.

Some people might suppose that William Temple and his fellow Commissioners did everything that was necessary in *Doctrine in the Church of England* when they wrote:

> No objection to a theory of evolution can be drawn from the two creation narratives in Gen. i. and ii. since it is generally agreed among educated Christians that these are mythological in origin, and that their value for us is symbolic rather than historical.[28]

That Temple's report has almost never been read is balanced by the fact that a good many other ordained Christians have spoken in the same sense. But this is pathetically too little! Recalling the words of Wolfgang Pauli, [29] we do not 'embrace' people by drawing no objection to them. By its derivation from the French, to embrace means that we throw our arms around and hug. This is now the only possible behaviour for Christian teachers in relation to evolution; and this because, for millions of our secular contemporaries, a glimmering reverence for the whole marvellous process will be the first step they will ever take in a religious direction.

Teilhard de Chardin wrote movingly on this theme; but many people, particuarly those who work within the ambience of science, have a deep antipathy for him. For this he is entirely to blame. Time and again he states or implies that his views are proved by scientific evidence when he

[28] *Op. cit:*, p.45
[29] See p. 32 above.

should have said no more than that they are not contradicted by anything known to the scientists. This error does not invalidate his more important conclusions. As long ago as in 1923, writing of the confusions of our century, he asked where we could find the light and the strength to follow the light? He answered: 'Only by...a clearer and more conscious faith in the supreme value of evolution.' On the following page he continued:

> So long as only their individual advantage seems to them at stake in earth's adventure . . . the men of our time will never submit their mind and will to anything greater than themselves. Explain to them unhesitatingly the greatness of the current of which they are a part . . . Compel them to see themselves as conscious elements in the complete mass of beings, inheritors of a labour as old as the world, and charged with transmitting the accumulated capital to all those who are to come. Then you will have overcome their tendency to inertia and disorder, and shown them *what they perhaps worshipped without giving it a name.*[30]

H'm! ' . . . only their individual advantage seems at stake in earth's adventure . . . ' It looks like a good definition of the splendid go-getter types on whom some of our irreligious Individualists would rely for the redemption of our society. By contrast, in his following sentences, Teilhard was descrbing the first moves towards religious Wholism. There is a great difference.

Teilhard also invited us to 'try, if only by some trick of the mind, to shift our outlook *unreservedly* into that of a world that is evolving.'[31] If we can really do this, far-reaching consequences for religious teaching will be seen to follow.

[30] *The Vision of the Past*, p. 76–7, my italics. Though the words were written in 1923, publication was vetoed by the Church until after Teihard's death, so they did not become available in English until published by Collins in 1966.

[31] *Christianity and Evolution* (Collins, 1971) p. 82, italics original.

Almighty and Omnipotent?

It was natural for the authors of the Bible, and for the leaders of the Church during its childhood, to believe and to say that God is Omnipotent and Almighty. In recent years I have read many pages in religious books designed to show that the two words are still acceptable *if we understand them in a special and erudite sense*. This is not good enough. In the privacy of their own hearts, people may give any meaning they like to the words they are thinking about. But, in a democratic age, great teaching institutions, in their public communications, must never use words except with the meanings that are attached to them in ordinary conversations among reasonably intelligent people. In such conversations, 'Almighty' and 'Omnipotent' describe someone, or Someone, who can do whatever he wants *now*. In this sense the words are deadly because they are untrue. God, or ultimate reality, or the Creator Spirit, always works within the limits imposed by the entire situation. For millions of years God could not have created a living cell. The preconditions had not been fulfilled. It needed millions more years before there could be monkeys. From these innocently but absolutely self-centred creatures, it was not possible for God to make a sinless man or woman, let alone a whole company of sinless men and women. Nor did he ever do so. Neither actually nor allegorically did the 'Fall of Man' ever happen. But it is upon the concept of this Fall that the Church now establishes its whole Christology of Redemption; and it is this which cannot be sustained in the light of our knowledge of evolution. ('Christology' may be roughly understood as the answer to the question: 'What is now the main work of Christ for his believers?') Today's Christology, with roots in the first chapters of Genesis, comes to us from Anselm (1033 – 1100 AD) who repudiated and transcended the far cruder Christology proposed by Irenaeus (130 – 200 AD). According to Irenaeus, the agonising death of his Son was the ransom price paid by God to the Devil so as to persuade him to release mankind from his otherwise invincible grip. If the Church could transform its Christology in the twelfth century, there is no reason why we cannot do it again now.

Anselm offered his answer to the basic question more than seven hundred years before evolution was even suspected. In those days men faced a baffling question: How could loving God have created sinful man? The question could only arise in societies that did not know about evolution. The only available answer at the time was that God created sinless men and women who then culpably 'fell' — fell into sin so deeply that there could be no at-one-ment between loving God and sinful Man until the innocent victim, Jesus Christ, suffered agonising death for our redemption.

I am aware that Christian scholars would say that a meticulous reading of Anselm shows his whole doctrine to have been more profound than my terse summary acknowledges.[32] But communication (or propaganda) from a huge teaching institution to millions of people is a rather blunt instrument; and it is no use saying that erudite study would reveal something slightly different from the generally received understanding. I have correctly stated the 'Message' which is now propagated from the Church and received by the 'average' church-goer. It will be painful to those who have learned to love the traditional teaching, but the fact is that the basic morality of this message would now be repudiated on every school playground from Vancouver to Vladivostock.

> To be our redeemer from death hell and sin
> Which Adam's transgression had wrappéd us in.

There is now no way in which such words as these can be even allegorically interpreted so as to make sense to an adolescent who knows about evolution.

Andrew Elphinstone wrote about the new possibilities or, as I would say, about the new necessities in his

[32] See, for example, Hans Küng *On being a Christian*, pp. 420–22.

wonderful book called *Freedom, Suffering and Love.* As an ordained minister, he wrote from an unchallengeably orthodox faith and showed that a far worthier religious understanding is available to us if we now surrender the idea that humanity has fallen from a one-time perfection, and accept the fact that we are, at this moment, the point that has been reached by life struggling upwards from the inter-tidal scum. The book was neither praised nor condemned by leaders of the Church. It was disturbing; so it was best to behave as if it hadn't happened.[33]

As we move into the early stages of our human adolescence, ideas about the Omnipotence of Almighty God actively close people's minds against religion of any kind. An example at a high level of erudition was displayed when Arthur Koestler discussed three books in which scientists explored the mysteries of life on earth. He found that the authors were looking towards 'a cosmic design — and hence a supreme designer'. At this exact point he turned away from the impossible. Increasing numbers of scientists, he said, might accept the first, but not the second — not 'a Designer who includes Auschwitz and the Gulag in his design.'[34] Nor are we concerned only for such men as Koestler looking at such enormities as the concentration camps. Every week, in more than one school in Britain, teachers have to meet pupils facing such a disaster as the death of a parent in a road crash. Almost everyone has a friend or acquaintance whose religious faith was strained or destroyed in a situation of similar character. 'Why did Almighty God let it happen?' The apparently unanswerable question falls off our shoulders as soon as we know that we live, not under the Power of Almighty God,

[33] Elphinstone's relatively early death was a real loss. His book includes very orthodox ideas about the objective existence of a personal Devil, which I believe has now become an irrelevant issue. It was published by SCM in 1976).

[34] Book review in the *Sunday Times*, 22.xi.81. The books were: *The View from Planet Earth* by Vincent Cronin; *A New Science of Life* by Rupert Sheldrake and *Evolution from Space* by Fred Hoyle and Professor Wickramasinghe.

but under the strong influence of the non-omnipotent Creator Spirit. This truth throws on us all a much greater load of personal responsibility. If God is Omnipotent, then let Him get on with it! But what if we are re-crucifying the non-omnipotent cosmic Christ whenever we do nothing about evils that could be mitigated if more people cared? The fact is that we live in a beautiful and fruitful but chancy and dangerous world. The dangers are caused mainly, but not wholly, by the blindness and greed of free humans. In this beautiful but dangerous world, the non-omnipotent Spirit calls on us to cooperate with her as bravely and as creatively as we can.

The Feminine in the Divine

The feminine pronoun is deliberate and necessary. Ever since its inception, the Christian religion has directed attention towards an exclusively male God. For almost half a millennium the Roman Catholics have had an edge over all Protestants and over almost all Anglicans in their adoration of Mary which brought femininity close to God. But we have reached a point at which 'close to' is not enough. The feminine needs to be carried into the heart of the Godhead — into the heart of ultimate reality, Deepest Truth or whatever translation anyone may prefer.

There is linguistic support for this view. The *Shekinah* (the Spirit of God) and the *Hagia Sophia* (the Wisdom of God) were both feminine words; as *Pneuma* the Spirit became neuter in Greek; in Latin, as *Spiritus Sanctus*, it became exclusively masculine. It seems rather hard. Women bear the whole of the arduous part in the unending recreation of human life on earth. And then we turn the Creator Spirit into a male! Our psychologists tell us that men and women alike combine male and female elements in their depths; and that we ought to try to keep a fair internal balance between the two. The masculinity of God during the childhood of the Christian Church has imposed an over-valuation on 'the typically masculine tendencies to coercion, domination, manipulation, retaliation, assertiveness, possessiveness, imperious over-riding power.' The West — and, because of the West, the whole world — desperately needs 'qualities traditionally regarded as feminine: gentleness, tenderness, compassion, receptiveness, intuition, humility, forbearance, long-suffering'.[35]

The Christology of the future will not be fully developed until large numbers of people come together with a more adolescent religious outlook. It is unreasonable to suppose that a single author could set it out completely. But already there are some pointers. Andrew Elphinstone, in his neglected book, made the amazing suggestion that Jesus, in his crucifixion, was not enabling God to accept culpably sinful man. Almost the opposite! He was enabling us to accept the non-omnipotent Creator Spirit who leaves us free and responsible, if we choose, to produce Auschwitz and the Gulag, and perhaps to destroy almost all life on earth. Teilhard de Chardin has explored in the same general direction. He wrote that the suffering Christ, without ceasing to be 'he who bears the sins of the world', indeed precisely as such, will become more and more in the eyes of believers 'he who bears and supports the weight of the world in evolution.'[36] It is too early to say where such explorations as these may lead. But something is already clear. Just as unequivocal repudiation of factual truth in physical miracles opens the door to a far more acceptable understanding of their spiritual significance, so the repudiation of Anselm's Christology will lead to a fuller understanding of the redeeming power of love.

[35] Quotations are from *Three Masks of the Tao*, by Joseph Needham, Published by the Teilhard Centre for the Future of Man in 1979. I am indebted to Needham for the whole of the last two paragraphs.
[36] *Christianity and Evolution* (Collins, 1971) p. 163.

5

To Fit Our Social State

In earlier days in Europe, and even now in other parts of the world, the Church won and wins its greatest successes amongst pagans. In our own country, until quite recently, it was addressing audiences who were quasi-pagans in that they or their children would have reverted to some kind of paganism if they had been left uninstructed. But pagans and quasi-pagans are religious people! Pagan children live in homes where the religious dimension of living is taken for granted in daily family conversations. Pagans are born into a religious attitude to life, almost as they are born with two eyes and ten toes. From the Christians' point of view, pagans believe in 'wrong' religions. The missionaries' strategy is simple: to proclaim the right religion — to proclaim Christ. In the past, the strategy did not always work. Many remained obdurately fixed in their pagan faith; but others were converted to Christianity. It is not suggested that this made no difference. To recall one of the greatest examples, the Cluniac Revival converted enough pagans, and the converts established and sustained a new kind of society. The point offered here is that when Christian teachers met pagans there was no inborn 'road block' obstructing the move from paganism to Christianity. The pagans were born with one religion; they moved over to a better religion.

There are still amongst us a minority with the same inborn religious attitude to life. For them, the obvious decision is to go to church. But, as John Robinson wrote: 'If Christianity is to survive, it must be relevant to modern secular man, not just to the dwindling number of the religious.'[1]

Here, as I see it, we find the most important example of the general tendency of churchmen to persist in their existing ways of teaching without bothering to ask themselves what has happened to the audience to which their message is addressed. Modern secular man is different from the huge company of past and present pagans, and from the recent quasi-pagans, not in degree, but in kind. He does not believe in 'wrong' religions. *He believes in no religion at all!* Unlike the sons and daughters of pagans, it is probable that in nine tenths of our homes, irrespective of social status, the children and adolescents do not hear a religious sentence spoken by their parents from one month's end to the next. It is almost certainly useless to 'proclaim Christ' to this huge secular majority. One might as well play concerts to the deaf or show pictures to the blind. Indeed teachers and preachers who extol Jesus to our typical secular people may be worse than useless. Their efforts could be counterproductive because it is painful for people to be 'instructed' in what they cannot possibly understand. We face entirely new questions which never arose when the Church faced pagans and quasi-pagans. What is involved in being a religious person? What does it mean to adopt a religious attitude to life? How do we now differentiate all the people who can be called religious from all who cannot? How can we describe the threshold that has to be crossed if one person is to move out of our almost universal religionless state so as to open himself or herself to religious possibilities? To answer such questions as these, we need a new basic affirmation of religious belief. Before offering any such affirmation, there needs to be a specification to show what some of its requirements will be.

The proposed affirmation must not include the word 'God' because it is now so deeply misunderstood that

[1] The *Observer*, March 17th 1963, two days before the publication of *Honest to God*.

anything depending on it will be misunderstood just as badly. It must not refer to Jesus because today's secular majority will not find anything special in him until after a genuine decision about there being a religious dimension in their own lives and in the life of the community. It must be simple so that almost anyone can understand it; and it must make the minimum possible demands so that the maximum number of people may be able to accept it as marking the transition from an irreligious to a religious way of life. But despite the simplicity of its minimum demands, it must have a real cutting edge so that today's hedonists and intellectuals and Individualists cannot accept it without knowing that they have found something deeper than the shallow purposes for which they are now living. As has been said already, it must be open to the Transcendent; but its immediate concern must be for the Truth within.[2]

It must point — perhaps no more than 'in a glass darkly' — to a possible world-wide development.

It must imply the fact, and the persistence, of evolution.

It must fit the underlying thought-and-feeling structure which is dominant in our day.

It will be seen that the specification is challenging. The earlier points can be left to stand on their own feet. The last three need to be considered more carefully.

In this book, the world situation can be considered only in a very superficial way. I can examine in some detail the British situation and, within it, the current teaching of Christianity, because this is the siutation and this the

[2] See pp. 60–61 above.

religious teaching that I would claim to know. Except in rudimentary ways, I do not know about other lands or about the teaching of other faiths. The world-wide challenge was set out by Arnold Toynbee who wrote:

> In our time, a cold war is being waged between all the ideologies on the one side and all the higher religions on the other side. This cold war is more momentous for the future of the human race than the family quarrel between two of the ideologies, Communism and Individualism, that is receiving so much attention today on both sides of 'the Iron Curtain'.[3]

The higher religions are therefore allies; and one of the bright lights in an otherwise mainly dark century has been the developing understanding, amongst many adherents of all religions, that they are not each others' enemies, but fellow seekers looking for the same mysterious truth from different starting points. Only those who want to rationalise their irreligion will feel that this world-wide fact is wholly annulled by followers of two versions of the Muslim faith in the Middle East and two variants of Christianity in Northern Ireland who still display the same sort of fratricidal lunacy as was widespread in European Christianity in the sixteenth and seventeenth centuries.

J. H. Oldham was being rather parochial when he described Salvation through Knowledge as being 'the most serious competitor of the Christian faith in the world today.'[4] I feel sure he would have agreed that it is now the most serious competitor of all the great religions of mankind. When the Europeans imposed themselves on the other civilisations, those others found themselves reluctantly obliged to look at the Europeans' ways. They were forced to do this in the first instance because it was so very obvious that the Europeans were much better at fighting. It was found that European superiority had

[3] *Change and Habit* (OUP, 1966) p. 171.
[4] See pp. 39–40 above.

nothing to do with religion, but depended entirely on science and technology. It was these that had to be copied. The difference between Christianity and the other religions is not that Christianity is attacked by the Religion of Science while the others are not; it is simply that the attack on Christianity was launched a few centuries earlier than the attack on the others. I write without detailed personal knowledge; but I am told that in the homelands of all the great traditions, the religious leaders are concerned by the fact that the local intellectual elite — even those who for expediency purport to accept the old religious faith — are less and less ready to accept it in its traditional dress.

Then what is to be done? At any relevant time, it is inconceivable that any one of the great religions will convert all or most of the people who now believe in the others. How can the higher religions express their alliance so that they know themselves to be fellow combatants against the ideologies? It is useless to look for any kind of amalgamation. There is no formula which could serve as a kind of lowest common denominator or highest common factor between, say, the Christian and the Muslim faith. Is it possible that there could be something describable as a religious 'ante-room'? Could there be a rather elementary affirmation which would involve the manifest repudiation of Salvation through Knowledge? Although such an affirmation would fall short of the full tenets of any of the traditional faiths, could it leave people open to advance into any one of them in the light of their own circumstances and experience? For sure, Christian teachers would hope that an acceptance of the basic affirmation would lead people to become Christians later on; and that would be my hope too. But if some were led to become Muslims, Buddhists, orthodox Jews or followers of some other faith, what of it? Allah and Jahweh and Gautama Buddha are all on the same side as Jesus against the brash materialism, the arid intellectualism and the rampant Individualism of our day.

From this world-wide point of view, I would therefore

repeat and re-emphasise a point that emerged from the consideration of our particular situation in Britain. We have reached a point in the spiritual development of humanity at which it is more important to know what differentiates religious from religionless people, more important to arouse people from a secular and into a religious attitude to life, than to convert them into professing followers of any particular faith. As has been suggested already, in our own country there is a good chance that those who take the first step will find that they become Christians later on.

If evolution is accepted by the ideologies, but rejected or treated ambiguously by the religions, the cold war will have been lost before it has even started. This means much more than an acceptance of evolution as a process which went on through millions of years in the past. Evolution is going on now! It seems almost arrogant to suppose that it ended as soon as our kind of animal came on the scene. For sure, it then ceased to depend on physical changes in the structure of the animals' bodies. When evolution made the astounding advance to creatures with a high level of self-consciousness, it persisted in the development of our skills, our knowledge, our ideas about ourselves and about our surroundings, our social organisation and institutions, and in everything to which these developments gave rise. In all these ways, evolution persists today and into the future. To suppose that evolution has reached its perfection in our day — or that it had reached it in the days of our Victorian ancestors — is a tempting idea for many. But — once more assuming for argument's sake that we do not soon destroy all life — how will this idea of ours appear to those who look back on it, say, from the middle of the fifth millennium? Will they not see our society as being riddled with a whole tangle of ideas and practices which they will regard as crazy — just as we do when we look back on some of the ideas and practices of the Middle Ages? A little more objectivity in our perception of the achievements of our immediate ancestors could be a valuable component in anyone's perception of life as a whole. The persistence of evolution in our present and future must be clearly implied in any basic affirmation which is to have any creative force today. If the ideologies treat evolution as something that ended several thousand years ago, while the religions see it as an on-going process, then in the end the ideologies will be the losers. Each will be asserting final perfection in its own ideas and institutions; and this will be increasingly at variance from the experience of ordinary people.

The last requirement for a basic religious affirmation is that it should fit the underlying thought-and-feeling structure which is prevalent in our day. In Europe and the Middle East there have been three different patterns of thinking and feeling in the last two thousand years: the Mythological, the Ontological and now the Functional. For more than one reason it is easier to label the three patterns than to describe them. To begin with, we know our separate items of knowledge and our moment-to-moment emotions much more immediately than we recognise an underlying structure holding them together in a pattern which we take for granted so readily that we seldom examine it. We are therefore discussing what is at most times little more than semi-conscious. For one person, any new item of knowledge simply attaches itself to the existing structure without changing it in any significant way. But what happens when an entire population is subjected to a continuing torrent of new knowledge, new understanding, new material products and new social institutions? No separate person is consciously aware of any sharp change in his or her underlying structure between the beginning of one week and the end of the next. But, in no more than a few decades, the deep thought-and-feeling structure of a whole people can change out of all recognition. It is too little to say that at the end of the period they have new things to know and think about. It is far more important that they have new ways of thinking and knowing.

An added difficulty comes from the fact that within the whole population some people and some families are affected by the on-going development much sooner than others. We do not respond simultaneously to the crack of a cosmic whip. Among our own population today, for example, there is still a modest minority who may know many of the separate items of the new knowledge without there having been as yet any deep change in the framework around which the items all cohere. This would be true of most of today's church-goers; and it has already been said that there is nothing morally wrong about their state. Despite our lack of full awareness, despite blurred edges and despite the long-drawn-out quality of the changes, there really have been three basic structures of thought and feeling in our part of the world in the last two thousand years.

Jesus lived and spoke and was heard in the Mythological Epoch. The mythological people of those days were sharply differentiated from ourselves in that they had not learned to separate the factual or historical aspects of any statement from its poetic or symbolic meaning. A keen Evangelical once challenged my denial of the objective existence of a personal Devil with words from the tenth chapter of St Luke's Gospel: 'I beheld Satan as lightning fall from heaven.' My opponent said that Jesus could not have seen him fall if he does not exist; and this arose because he could not believe that he lived with a basic thought structure wholly different from that of Jesus and his contemporaries. It never occurred to Jesus that his hearers would suppose that his outward, or even his inward, eye had actually seen an objectively existing Being plunging downward in a flash of light. He meant, and his hearers knew that he meant, much the same as we should understand if someone said: 'I suddenly knew that in the end evil cannot win.'

Because Jesus spoke and thought in the mythological age, it follows that there have always been strong mythical elements in the Christian message and in the faith of every Christian believer. There is nothing wrong in this; on the contrary, it can be an advantage because mythological language and imagery can often carry the truth to deeper levels of our being than those that could be reached by the more exact wording of our day. The fatal error is to condemn mythological statements by applying ontological concepts so as then to dismiss the truth itself.

An outstanding feature of the Ontological Epoch — indeed the one that gave it its name — was a deep concern for existence and for substance. No matter what they were thinking about, the people of that age wanted to know how its existence was to be apprehended; of what substance was it made? Was everything made of fire, air, earth and water? Or did it, as Democritus guessed, ultimately reduce to tiny discrete and indivisible atoms? (Atomos = Indivisible) In fewest words, whatever they thought about, they asked: 'What is it?' The object of their thought stood there, inactive and unrelated and uninvolved; and they wanted to know what it was.

Hans Küng, in the book already quoted, considered the argument which has caused such division since the sixteenth century around the word 'is' in the sentence translated as 'This is my body'. He rightly wrote that the argument has been irrelevant because neither the early Christian community, 'nor Jesus himself, had our concept of a substance. People did not ask what a thing was, but what it was for; not in what it consisted, but what was its function.'[5] We shall find that a very big wheel has now come full circle.

In the fourth century the Roman Empire was torn by a controversy with the Arians; and Constantine had to call a conference at Nicaea to try to settle it. The orthodox insisted that Jesus is 'of the same substance as the Father': the Arians would go no further than that he is 'of a like substance'. The orthodox victory became an integral part of the Nicaean Creed which we used until very recent

[5] *Op. cit:* p. 325. See footnote p. 36 above.

times. To the modern mind and, one would suppose, to the mind of Jesus, it would be quite difficult to find an issue less important. This does not mean that the men who met at Nicaea were stupid or insincere. It does mean that the structure of their thinking was different from ours, and different from that of the people who actually heard Jesus speaking.

In the thirteenth century, Thomas Aquinas offered four famous proofs of the existence of God, and other great writers of the Ontological Epoch have offered others. We have already considered the proof offered by Archdeacon Paley less than two hundred years ago. All these proofs have now been demolished as anyone who is interested can confirm by reading *The Miracle of Theism*[6]. Many people who read the demolitions — and far larger numbers who hear about them rather vaguely — suppose that they are being told about the total irrelevance of religion. They are not. They are being told that we no longer live in the Ontological Epoch.

The Functional epoch can be dated from the 1770's. Until then it had been supposed that fire was a *substance* (phlogiston) which *existed* in wood, coal, sulphur and other materials so that it could be caused to escape by suitable treatment. Then Priestley and Lavoisier co-operated and competed to show that fire is not a substance and does not 'exist' at all. Fire is a process in which billions of billions of molecules are changing their relationships to each other and thereby setting up further processes one of which, after passing through our eyeballs, enables us to say, quite correctly: 'A fire is burning on the hearth.' This was the first example of the functional pattern of thinking which now dominates our daily working lives.

For example, heat and light and sound do not exist in

[6] By J. L. Mackie, published by OUP in 1982.

today's meaning of the word. They are processes which establish relationships between ourselves and our environment. Time and gravity do not exist; but bad luck to those who think they can ignore their rules. It was correct to say that evolution, more than anything else in the last hundred and fifty years, has turned our world upside down; but it does not exist. It is a process which involves changed relationships between creatures and their successors and their environment. Michael Faraday and James Clerk Maxwell 'discovered' electromagnetism, and without it the life of the twentieth century would come to a shuddering halt in much less than a week. Yet it does not exist. Psychology and psychiatry do not exist. Their practitioners are involved in processes which may change people's relationship to themselves, to each other and to life as a whole. Within my own expertise, propaganda does not exist; but the fact stands out that as a process it can affect, for good or ill, the relation of people to everything that goes on.

Books are being written in our time which ascribe the change in our thought structures to the work of the great physicists earlier in our century.[7] This cannot be right because the transformation was well advanced before they started work. But the contemporary scientists are crucially important. In earlier writing, I quoted Frederick Stokes who described himself and his contemporaries as:

> we who live in times when the Church is traversing the vast desert which separates the devout faith of the past from the baptised science of the future.[8]

The astonishing fact is that this was written in 1889.[9] The sad fact is that the leaders of the Church have not been traversing the vast desert. They have been fixed on its backward rim by minorities who threatened institutional

[7] See, for example, Fritjof Capra, *The Tao of Physics* and *The Turning Point* (Wildwood House, 1975 & 1982).
[8] *We Teach Them Wrong* p. 4.
[9] In an Introduction to Maitland's *Dark Ages*.

disturbance if their leaders explored to find contemporary ways of expressing traditional truth. But now the scientists themselves are beginning to express the baptised science of the future. This was described for non-scientists by Professor Keith Ward in broadcasts in the spring of 1986.[10] He quoted Dr Peacocke as saying:

> The scientists show us a world in which things are interconnected; processes at one level manifest themselves as events at other levels. There is a continuous web of interconnection across space and through time in the development of the cosmos.[11]

Walter Schwarz, religious editor of the *Guardian*, discussed Ward's book, and several others written in the same sense, and commented:

> It does not follow from this argument that people should be flocking back into the churches. These appear firmly stuck in the musty idiom of a pre-scientific world.[12]

The fact is that increasing numbers of scientists, starting from their scientific understanding, come close to the mystics of all religions who have always known and said that we and all the apparently separated items around us are inter-related in a single whole. The scientists describe their findings in process-and-relationship language, and not in the language of substance-and-existence.

It should be noticed that in all the phenomena that have been considered there is always something that 'exists' in the everyday meaning of the word, even though scientists would tell us that the 'something' ultimately resolves into photons, pions, muons, quarks and other mysteries comprehensible only in the scientists' process-and-relationship language. But, for example, with light the glass bulb and the wire filament exist in our ordinary use

[10] Now expanded and published by the BBC as *The Turn of the Tide*.
[11] *Op. cit:* p. 39
[12] *Op. cit:* in the first of two feature articles, October 27–28th 1987.

of the word; in sound: the violin string or whatever else; in propaganda: the printed leaflet and the television transmitter; and so on. But in every instance, that which can be said to exist is the relatively unimportant. What really matters — what produces the result — is the process that affects relationship. Each of these processes is a component in ultimate reality. In our understanding of words, it is acceptable to say that they are real. But — again in our understanding of words — it cannot be said that they *exist*.

This being our attitude to so much that so closely affects and even determines our everyday lives, and this being our way of understanding it, why does the Church seem to be asking us whether we believe in the *existence* of God? Collectively, the leaders of the Church allow us to suppose that this is the key question which separates the religious from the irreligious. 'Do you believe in the existence of God?' 'Yes': you are religious; 'Don't know': you are agnostic; 'No': you are atheist. Within today's underlying thought structures, a majority of our contemporaries cannot give a confident affirmative answer to what seems to be the Church's watershed question. They therefore class themselves as religionless people, and thereby close themselves against their own spiritual growth. They are left with their intellects and their emotions; and apart from conclusions that might be reached on theoretical grounds, the mass media are showing us that this has turned us into an increasingly sick society.

It may be said that we are only arguing about words; and in a sense this could be true. I am told that a philosopher has shown that substance-and-existence language and process-and-relationship language meet on common ground if both are pressed to their limits. But I will not allow 'only-arguing-about-words' to be used as if we are discussing what hardly matters. Words, at any moment in our social development, are immensely powerful and important; and to ignore them can lead to disaster. Indeed, at the end of the second chapter, I described how a single word — or rather the absence of a single letter from a word — could deprive us of a concept that was essential for our social development. Those who are trying to teach the truth must continuously re-examine the words they are using to see whether they are still conveying, or whether they are now obscuring, the underlying reality. If they are obscuring it, they have to be changed.

Once we know that in our day the starting point should be with the immanent Truth, it ought not to be too difficult to describe it in process-and-relationship thought forms. This will open the way to the possibility of knowing the transcendent Truth as well. It will rescue us from the dead end which is reached today when people continue to address us in the language of the ontological age in which substance and existence determined the shape of our ancestors' thinking.

It is a significant, though relatively minor, matter that the end of the ontological age frees us from the old argument about the objective existence of the Devil. When we know that we work with a process-and-relationship substructure, the reality of evil is obvious in ourselves and our family relationships, in social and international affairs, and in the total situation that is now imposed on us by our ancestors and our history. In ourselves and in our families, we have to come to terms with its reality. In the outside world we have to contend against it as if it were a personal enemy.

The change that I am proposing is bound to disturb some of today's church-goers. For hundreds of years they and their ancestors have worshipped Our Father. If this Father does not 'exist' in any contemporary meaning of the word, they will see themselves as being told that their faith has been in vain. Nothing of the kind. They can be assured that their ancestors were not wrong, that they themselves are not wrong, and that no one is trying to convert them. It is natural that a minority should remain in the ontological age when majorities have moved into the functional. If their religious faith is sustained by their substance-and-existence thought forms, why should anyone quarrel? A quarrel can only arise if they turn around and tell us that we are wrong to have adopted the thought forms of the functional age. If the quarrel were pressed, we could ask about fourteen verses in the Book of Psalms where Ultimate Reality is described as 'My Rock'. Jesus knew the Psalms by heart. Is it to be supposed that he performed a mental operation describable as believing in the objective existence of a cosmic rock? Of course not. 'My Rock' and 'Our Father', when spoken in the mythological or in the functional age, describe a relationship between us and God — or between us and whatever translation of the difficult word anyone may prefer. In this and in other ways the mythical and the functional epochs are far more akin to each other than is either to the ontological age which separated them in time. One recalls Hans Küng's comment on the mythological thinking of Jesus and his contemporaries and the ontological thinking of those who lived through most of the centuries which constituted the childhood of the Christian Church.[13]

The specification for a basic religious affirmation has now been set out. It would have been better if its requirements had been met by the cooperative work of a number of concerned people. I must do my best without such help.

> *Each of us may be perceived as a tiny conscious cell within a far greater Whole. There is therefore a relationship between the process going on in each and the far greater process that goes on all around. The relationship between the two is, from one side, attraction, invitation, call or challenge; and from the other, affection, response and seriously attempted cooperation. By offering or by withholding our care and attention, we can to some extent promote or inhibit the development of this relationship.*

[13] See p. 79 above.

This single paragraph could stand on its own. It contains the core of the matter. If people seriously look into their depths and accept the sense of this paragraph (not necessarily the exact words) as an accurate description of themselves and of their relationship to all else, then, in my view, they will have crossed the threshold from an irreligious to a religious way of life. But there ought to be a second paragraph to spell out some of the consequences which flow from the first. Once again, it is the general sense, and not the exact language that counts.

> *Both inside and outside, if the process moves healthily, this development leads towards greater consciousness and greater unity. The challenge or call to each is therefore to persist towards greater consciousness and unity on the inside, and to find greater involvement in the process outside. This invites us to perceive, as best we may, the point that has been reached by the outside process now, so that we can be useful to it insofar as it has made itself known to us. We shall be led to some kind of service to others grounded on love. At some point we shall surely meet pain and loss. We may meet what the secular world will call total defeat.*

Many of today's church-goers will complain that the proposed religious affirmation is poor anaemic stuff compared to the full-blooded faith, the creative and personal relationship, which inspires and guides their lives. They will dismiss it as regurgitated Humanism. Most of them will see here a double statement of the same overwhelming argument. In fact there are two quite different criticisms and they need to be met in two almost opposite ways.

Poor anaemic stuff compared to a full and sincere belief in the whole Christian truth; or, for that matter, compared to a profound belief in any other of the great religious traditions? *Of course!* The proposed affirmation defines a starting point, not a destination. It will be recalled that an important part of its specification was that it should make the minimum demands so that the maximum number of people should be able to accept it as marking the watershed between an irreligious and a religious attitude to life. If people will start from here, they will approach their destinations later on. All are open to become Christians. If some are attracted to some other tradition, it will not be a spiritual disaster. It will be sad if others live their lives without any developments or experiences which carry them beyond the starting point. But even these will have escaped from the irreligious ambience of contemporary Britain.

Then what of the other criticism? Is this nothing more than regurgitated Humanism? The orthodox are likely to see it as such. Although many of them take a more balanced view, it is probable that a majority of today's church-goers — like a majority of the whole population in the not very distant past — are far more comfortably involved with 'God out there' than with a search for Truth which starts within themselves. We have seen already that a huge majority of our contemporaries are constituted in the opposite way; and that a recent Archbishop of Canterbury, when addressing an audience drawn mainly from this majority, found it perfectly proper to begin with 'what is going on inside you.'[14] But, to most of today's church-goers, this would constitute a turning away from God whom they know and love. To them, the procedure approved by the Archbishop looks like a move towards what is human, and for this reason they would condemn it as regurgitated Humanism.

In fact it is nothing of the kind. Humanism is UDI on behalf of the human race — a Unilateral Declaration of Independence. Humanists see us all as independent of anything greater than ourselves. Most of them see human intellect as a sufficient instrument for social progress. In this sense, Humanism is a glorification of Man. For sure there have been altruistic Humanists and there are still large numbers of them today. Indeed, despite contri-

[14] See p. 59 above.

butions from well known Christians such as Wilberforce, Shaftesbury and George Lansbury, these altruistic Humanists have been the main instruments of social improvement for more than a hundred years. Many church-goers are put to shame if they remember that 'it is not those who say to me "Lord, Lord", who will enter the Kingdom of heaven, but the person who *does the will* of my Father in heaven.'[15] Despite this, I have suggested already that the events of recent years raise the question whether Humanism is tough enough for the job in hand.[16] In a sense opposite from that which applies to Humanism, the proposed affirmation can also be seen as a glorification of Man. Alone among creatures, humans have not been created so as only to promote their own satisfactions and to perpetuate their species; they have been created so as to serve and to participate in a far greater purpose.

The proposed affirmation is not offered for intellectual judgment based on social calculation. It is not the same kind of thing as the frequent assertion that modern technology has made the planet into a unity and that we should therefore be better off if more people tried to establish some kind of world-wide regulatory institutions. In ancient language, it is offered to each separate person for acceptance 'with all your heart, and with all your soul, and with all your mind, and with all your strength.' Acceptance or rejection does not at all depend on any calculation about what might or might not happen if it were or were not accepted by other people; it depends on the answer to the question: 'In the last analysis, what am I?' It is a suggestion that we should cut ourselves down to size by knowing that we are nothing more than tiny cells within a far greater Whole. At the same time it is an invitation to see our significance and purpose by knowing that we are nothing less than contributory cells within something almost infinitely greater. Apart from the very small minority whose brains are seriously disordered, there is not one of us who

[15] Matthew 7.21. Jerusalem Bible translation, my italics.
[16] See pp. 1–2 above.

cannot contribute something to the good health of the area which his or her influence can reach. This is more or less the same thing as any healthy cell does in any animal's body.

Other people may look at the proposed affirmation and complain that they have heard it all before. This can be answered very shortly. *Of course they have!* There is no new religion waiting to be invented. There are only the familiar insights to be re-asserted in the thought-forms of our day.

Orthodox believers may complain that the affirmation contains no element of mystery. For sure, it does not include any of the conventional mystery language. But does that mean no mystery? What of the first sentence? Biologists would say that every healthy cell in a healthy body is cooperating to sustain the well being of the whole creature. But these cells, though living and containing lives, are not conscious in any ordinary meaning of the word. They cooperate whether they want to or not. By contrast, humans are conscious beings — indeed highly self-conscious. We can make decisions with whatever liberty we have. It is only too obvious that we are not all cooperating to promote the good health of the Whole. In twos and threes, in hundreds and thousands, and even in tens and hundreds of millions, we are furiously antagonistic to each other; and far too many of us live in comfort or even in luxury partly or wholly by exploiting others. As shown to us by television camera crews, the whole thing looks much more like a multi-partite civil war than like any kind of unity. Yet the assertion is offered: 'Each of us may be perceived as a tiny conscious cell within a far greater Whole'. In the late twentieth century, people can begin to live religiously without any other mystery than this.

There is, however, a further mystery in the second sentence. We are all linked to the eternal and we can become aware of it to some extent if we choose to expose ourselves to the possibility. We can play our tiny parts in what 'was in the beginning, is now and ever shall be.' These words can seem to exclude part of the entire wisdom of our society if they are taken to mean that 'in the beginning' every species of plant and animal was just the same as it 'is now'. But what if we add an evolutionary dimension to the time-honoured words? They would then assure us that we have emerged from a process which started 'in the beginning' while the preconditions for the first living cells were slowly evolving on the lifeless planet; which has continued ever since, is persisting now and will go on into the future unless we end it in nuclear war.

It can be added that we are all mysteriously cell-like in that after a time our bodies die, though some of us live longer than others. The same is true of the cells in our bodies. Their whole life span varies. 'Average cells' (if such a concept makes sense) live less than seven years, and many die much younger. They are simultaneously being replaced by others. Yet it is obvious to me that I am the same person — in a sense I am the same process — as when I was a child. This seems very strange.

There are two advantages in perceiving the mysterious element in the proposed affirmation and in the whole situation in which we live. The lesser is that it differentiates religious people from those who claim to be living in accordance with ethical principles. Many of these are good people who work for good causes. But the principles of ethics, though not so certain as those of mathematics, are far too intellectual to give us back 'that which the living religions of every age have given to their believers.'[17] The intellectual principles of ethics will not reach deeply enough to sustain healthy and creative societies. There has to be the mysterious — the unprovable and the undisprovable — confronting us in our depths with the childlike question: 'Does it feel as if it's true?' This recalls words attributed to Jesus and spoken in the mythological language of his day: 'Whosoever shall not receive the kingdom of God as a little child shall in no wise enter therein.'[18]

[17] See p.11 above.
[18] Luke 18.17

The other and greater advantage in recognising the mysterious element in our situation is that we are then emotionally enabled, but not intellectually compelled, to move from the immanent truth — from an understanding of what we actually are in our depths — so as to find our way of making contact with the transcendent Truth as well. This will be considered more closely in a later chapter.

Meanwhile it is important to notice that the basic affirmation is offered in language which is not necessarily personal nor necessarily impersonal. Indeed, at this particular moment in the spiritual development of humanity, I would regard 'Personal' as a rather dangerous word. It triggers a thought-association process: 'Personal' → 'a person' → 'a Person with a big capital "P" ' → 'a Big Invisible Man.' And then, because we know that the Basic Truth is nothing of the kind, we are given an easy rationalisation for dismissing religion as a whole from our serious concern. The personal-impersonal way of looking at religious truth is supported by Arnold Toynbee who wrote:

> My guess is that the ultimate spiritual reality behind the everyday world in which most of us are living during most of our lifetime is both personal and impersonal and is also neither personal nor impersonal. I cannot think of It as being 'God' or 'the Gods', because these words imply something that is wholly and solely personal. I can think of It as being the Holy Spirit, and I believe It is human-like, not in being a personality like a human being, but in being non-omnipotent like a human being. I fancy that 'omnipotent' is a meaningless word, but anyway I do not believe that the reality can be both omnipotent and good, and I do not believe that It is evil. I believe It is trying, as we try, to make things better.[19]

[19] In a letter to the author on April 26th 1973. The same view has no doubt been expressed in Toynbee's other writing. This letter brought the understanding that it is wrong to describe the ultimate spiritual reality as omnipotent in the ordinary meaning of the word.

Orthodox traditionalists may dismiss Toynbee who was never one of their number. I would therefore support the personal-impersonal quality of the proposed affirmation with significant words from W. R. Matthews, Dean of St Paul's from 1936 to 1967, and one of the most orthodox Anglicans of our century. He wrote that 'there are moments of religious insight which everyone would call religious but which neither suggest nor imply the presence of a personal God.' He described 'states of the soul which are elements in any religious consciousness, but do not, as such, contain the immediate suggestion of a personal response.' In a footnote he set out Addison's well known lines about the stars:

> In reason's ear they all rejoice
> And utter forth in glorious voice:
> For ever singing as they shine,
> 'The hand that made us is Divine'.

On these lines Matthews wrote that the contemplation of the starry heavens may induce a religious emotion which has no tendency to invoke the thought of a Creator; 'nor', he added, 'does the religiousness of the contemplation depend necessarily on hearing the voice "in reason's ear" proclaiming "the hand that made us is Divine".'[20]

Matthews quite rightly, insisted in his immediately following pages, that the huge majority of Christians in the past and still today, found and find a very strong personal element in their faith. His quoted words are offered to support the view that belief in 'a Person' is not an indispensible part of a religious attitude to life. Humanists must be described as irreligious if they are still enthralled by Logical Positivism, or by any of its variants, because its criteria reduce the first decisive sentences of the proposed affirmation to insignificance. But Humanists can be described as religious if they accept these sentences, even

20 *God in Human Thought and Experience* (Nisbet & Co, 1930) pp. 159–60.

though they accept them in impersonal terms. If some Christians want to think of them as religious beginners, so be it. It is crazy, at this moment in the spiritual development of humanity, to drive them away by telling them that they are not religious at all.

The proposed affirmation is not a *diktat*. It is offered to those who will accept it. Nor is it eternal truth, because eternal truth does not change. It is a way of pointing to the truth in words and concepts that may be acceptable today. It would have been impossible two hundred years ago, and may be out of date in a hundred years time. It is offered, nevertheless, as a way in which we can today distinguish between all who are religious and all who are not. Those who accept it, including those who accept it as a minor consequence of a deeper faith, are to be counted as religious. Those who do not know whether they can accept it are agnostics. Those who reject it must be regarded as secular or religionless. It must be obvious that those who start by accepting the proposed affirmation — or by accepting something like it — will be open to receive the essence of Christian truth if it comes to them later on in the light of their experience.

6

Individualists and Wholists

From the beginning of the book I have made it clear that I reject Individualism. In its earliest centuries it was a creative religious cause, wresting basic freedom from Authority. It has become an ideology wholly unsuited to the society that it has brought into being. Some readers may have agreed; some will have been doubtful; others will have been antagonised by what they read. The question must be considered more carefully.

Throughout our century, Individualists have claimed — or, much more powerfully, they have been able to imply without being obliged openly to assert — that we are all Individualists now because we all oppose the Authoritarians. Individualism, they would have suggested, is the basis of our western Freedom; we fought for it against the Nazis; we must be ready to defend it against the Authoritarians of our day. It may well be that this is the semi-conscious reason why almost all our best educated people stay publicly silent in face of the rampaging Individualism of our go-getter types, and of the gentler materialism which dominates the lives of our vast middling majority.

I believe that this goes back to the spelling mistake made by Jan Smuts in 1928. *He left us with no acceptable word for the other kind.* It is not true that all who oppose the Authoritarians have to be Individualists; and those who suggest it are hiding one of the most divisive human chasms under a paper-thin layer of verbal error. 'Individualists' is the wrong name for all the opponents of the Authoritarians. They may be described as Democrats or, more accurately and in a rather ugly word, as Pluralists. All Pluralists oppose the idea that people should be told what to believe and think and do by an authoritarian Church or State. All agree that people should be free to make their basic decisions and to develop their personalities in their own ways. It is after making these basic common judgments that people have to face the chasm. Everyone has to answer the question: *Are you an Individualist or a Wholist?* Teilhard de Chardin described the choice as being between

> Two possibilities determining two basic attitudes, more radical then any difference of race, nationality or even formal religion; and between them runs the true line of the spiritual division of the Earth.

Teilhard, when writing in 1936 (or perhaps his translator working in the early 1960s) chose one-word descriptions of the two different kinds of people which do not seem best fitted to the 1980s. But his descriptions of them are perfectly clear. For Individualists:

> The world is moving in the direction of dispersal and therefore of the growing autonomy of its separate elements. For each individual the business, the duty and the interst of life consist in achieving, in opposition to others, his own utmost uniqueness and personal freedom; so that perfection, beatitude, supreme greatness belong not to the whole but to the least part.

Wholists see themselves in an entirely different way. As Teilhard put it:

> For the elements of the world to become absorbed within themselves by separation from others, by isolation, is a fundamental error. The individual, if he is to fulfil and preserve himself, must strive to break down every kind of barrier which prevents separate beings

> from uniting. His is the exaltation, not of egoistical autonomy, but of communion with all others.[1]

The choice to be made by any one person does not depend on detailed speculation about probable or possible future consequences. Each has to give his or her answer to basic religious questions: 'What sort of creature are you? What sort of creatures should humans see themselves to be?' Nevertheless we are facing the choice between two attitudes to life where the difference is at least as great as the difference between the followers of Hengist and Horsa and those of Archbishop Lanfranc; at least as great as the difference between the men who created Massachusetts and those who, in the same centuries, sustained Spain. Though I was little more than sleep-walking at the time, I can now see with hindsight that this is what I dimly had in mind more than forty years ago when I wrote that 'no organisation of society could be run successfully by the sort of people we were in 1939.'[2]

The scientists, as we saw, are finding that 'there is a continuous web of interconnection across time and space in the development of the cosmos.' Can the Individualists be right in supposing that the rule of basic interconnection is suddenly reversed when the cosmos develops to the level of men and women, so that real significance now resides, not in the whole, but in each of the separate parts? It looks as if the Individualists' ideology is not only an impossible way of harmoniously managing our industrial society. Perhaps it is also unscientific!

Individualists reveal themselves by the inner shudder which comes through into the tone of voice in which they speak the words 'vast mass'. Their Individualism appears in their almost pathological hatred of the State which, with all its faults, is nothing more or less than all of us when we try to organise ourselves for something that we regard as a common purpose. 'I claim my rights as an Individual!'

[1] *The Future of Man*, first published in English by Collins in 1964; my quotations are from the Fontana edition of 1969, pp. 47–8.
[2] See p. 5 above.

I have sometimes surprised one of the claimants by pointing out that, as such, he or she is absolutely entitled to what could be scratched up from raw nature by teeth and fingernails. Anything more than that depends absolutely on membership of an immensely complex and necessarily costly Whole which has been brought to its present state by millennia of social endeavour. On this basis, Individualists are wholly wrong when they imply that taxation is a form of robbery; as are also the owners of newspapers when they get their writers openly to applaud the cunning of lawyers and accountants who enable very rich men to evade the 'Death Duty' laws which have been sustained by governments of every colour for about a hundred years. Taxation means that we return, to the Whole, a relatively small part of what we could not have had at all if it did not sustain us.

For Wholists, the development of their personalities can go forward only by involvement in, and communion with, all the hundreds and thousands and millions of other people by whom we are surrounded. It goes further than to our fellow men and women. We feel an involvement in the whole of the little planet — mineral, vegetable, animal and human — on which it is our amazing privilege to be alive. This will be considered more carefully at a later stage.

Individualists do not understand that in the last five hundred years the caravan has moved on. Half a millennium ago, it had to be asserted that men and women could not be fully human unless they made their basic decisions for themselves. The possibility or, as many said at the time, the absolute certainty that large numbers would make wrong decisions, seemed less intolerable than that decisions should be imposed by Authority. Today Wholists would assert that they cannot be fully human unless they make their free decisions about the ways in which they will offer themselves back in service to the Whole on which they depend for everything they have — in service to the eternal purpose that has been at work since before ever the first living cells were formed.

This is not a matter of personal choice as when one says 'I like Brahms' and another 'I like Pop'. We are confronting a matter of fact. For sure we are free to reject the fact if we wish. This is where human freedom begins. If we were not free to make a wrong choice, we should draw no strength from making the right one. But, *as a matter of fact*, humans *are* tiny conscious cells whose freedom is to choose how to contribute to the eternal. (Or they may be described in other words in which someone else might express the same basic meaning.) 'I am far more important than a tiny conscious cell' is a statement of the same quality as 'I am much taller than Nelson on the top of his column.'

Part of the specification for the basic religious affirmation was that, although simple, it was to have a sharp cutting edge so that today's Individualists could not accept it without knowing that they had found something deeper than the shallow purposes for which they are now living.[3] This was achieved in the first sentence. Individualists do not perceive themselves as tiny conscious cells within a far greater Whole. For each Individualist, he or she *is* the purpose of existence. I hope that some who have previously described themselves as Individualists — perhaps because of seeing no other way of making a stand against the Authoritarians — will now realise that they have in fact been Wholists all the time. Those who remain Individualists, even when the Wholist alternative has been described to them, must now be regarded as irreligious people *even if they attend church services*. This judgment may be wrong. But it must not be dismissed simply because it would seem un-Christian to tell some of today's church-goers that their attitude to life is not religious. Respectable synagogue-goers were told the same thing a long time ago. Historians of a distant future will see the necessity for Individualism, and will therefore recognise its religious qualities, in its early creative stages. But they will be surprised by its long association with Christianity. The much cited care of Jesus for each separate person

[3] See p. 73 above.

never meant that he wanted each to be separated from everyone else or from the community as a whole. On the contrary, he prayed 'that they all may be one.'[4] Individualists are terrified that if all are one then each will lose that which differentiates him or her from all the others. They are answered in two devastating words: 'Union differentiates!'[5] The organs of our bodies are differentiated from each other, not in spite of, but because of their union in one body. St Paul used this fact as an analogy in one of his letters.[6]

[4] John 17–21.
[5] Teilhard de Chardin, *Human Energy*, (Collins, 1969) p. 64.
[6] I Corinthians 12.

7

A Speculation

Acceptance or rejection of a religious affirmation cannot hang on any calculation about its probable or possible social consequences.[1] It is wrong to say that people should, or must, accept some suggested belief *because* favourable changes would be more likely if they did. The decision must turn on whether the affirmation seems true in its own right. The basic affirmation offered in this book depends on whether people see themselves as tiny conscious cells within an infinitely greater eternal process. Or do they insist that their *individual* significance is far greater than that?

Nevertheless it seems legitimate to come at the question the other way round so as to speculate about some of the long term social consequences that might follow if, hypothetically, there came a time when large numbers of people had agreed to the affirmation simply because they had accepted its truth. In this chapter there is an additional and personal reason for my treating the theme as a speculation: 'there is something wrong about me as I naturally stand'. For more than half a century I have believed that we shall eventually have to establish the Common Ownership of all land and of all the great productive resources;[2] and it is wrong to believe that long advocacy of any cause gives one an increased assurance of being right. The opposite could be more nearly true. If anyone supports a cause through several decades, deep emotional forces are built up in its favour. These, through 'Original Sin', then

[1] See pp. 88–96 above.
[2] See pp. 2–3 above.

admit into conscious mind the facts and arguments that support the cause; and they keep the others out. Fortunately we are not required to be cocksure, but only to 'perceive as best we may' so as to be useful to the eternal purpose 'in so far as it has made itself known to us.'

It will be worth while to look at the total defeat of 'Nationalisation' which, from the Labour Party's inception in 1900, was the only proposal which distinguished it from the left-wing Liberals of the day. There were two significant but minor failures springing from the fact that propagandists cannot pick and choose the meanings that shall be attached to their important words; they have to accept the meanings that spring to people's minds and reverberate in their emotions when the words are heard or read. This made it disastrous for Labour's advocates to claim that they would 'abolish Capitalism and establish Socialism'. When people meet the word 'Socialism', the reverberation for many decades has been 'What-they-have-in-Russia'. In reasonably intelligent conversations, 'Capitalism' actually means tens of thousands of little firms with anything from two to two hundred employees where the owners go down every day and work at managing their little businesses. Such firms will persist and fill up the gaps in any imaginable future society; and if some people doubt it, they should read *The Economic of Feasible Socialism*[3] or, for that matter, they should look at some of the things that Gorbachov is trying to do in Russia. The real intention is far better displayed by saying that some day we shall have to end Corporationised Society and establish the Common Ownership Community. Recent developments raise the question whether our existing social structure should not be better described as Conglomerate Society.

But there was a far deeper reason for the defeat of Nationalisation. Despite all the glorious writing of R. H. Tawney, Labour propagandists said or — exactly the same thing — they seemed to say that in each separate industry Nationalisation would bring greater efficiency, higher

[3] Alec Nove (George Allen & Unwin, 1983).

output and profit for the nation. To each voter, except to the tiny minorities who owned each industry in question, the Labour Party was saying: 'Nationalisation will make you better off'. Socialism was being commended for the Individualists' reasons! Contrary to what we were persistently told in the press, careful research has shown that the nationalised industries were probably run rather more efficiently than the others. But Labour had not said 'probably rather better'; Labour had said 'certainly far better'. And it did not happen.

Hence the devastating words of G. D. H. Cole at a fringe meeting during the Labour Party Conference at Margate in 1948:

> It is very difficult to win a majority for a socialist programme when the people don't want Socialism; and they don't — not unless they think it would make them better off; and it wouldn't — not in terms of anything that they now understand by those words.

So far as I know, Cole lived his life as a beneficent Humanist. But in those words he was saying that there could be no Common Ownership Community except through a religious change in the outlook of the people. This is what makes it worth while to look at what seems like a political question in a book about religion.

Contrary to what I said, or seemed to say, in the 1940s, the legislated establishment of the Common Ownership Community would not, of itself, do anything to improve any sense of social responsibility in the people. This must not now be timidly admitted; it must be resolutely proclaimed. If there is to be a change from our religionless Individualism, it has to be promoted and directed from some other source. When this has been asserted, two facts stand out. If there were to be an increasingly articulated determination that we should at some time establish the Common Ownership Community, this would immediately improve the chance that more people would adopt a more socially responsible, and a less individualistic, attitude to life. By contrast, if we have to work on the basic assumption that Corporationised (or Conglomerate) Society is to persist for ever, then the chance for increased social responsibility is bound to be almost immeasurably reduced. For this there are two related reasons.

If every important economic and industrial decision depends on some group of rich men who ask what it will mean to 'their' corporation; if, floating above these men, there is the increasing power of take-over bidders and other property manipulators who deflect industrial managers from the wise long-term conduct of their corporations and force them to go for short-term share valuation depending on maximising immediate dividends; if far more than 90% of our best educated people see all this as arising out of the permanently desirable structure of our society; then what hope is there that those in the middle and at the bottom of the social pile will run their own lives otherwise than on 'What-do-I-and-my-kind-get-out-of-it'? To the surprise of many soul-saving church-goers, this is a religious question. It determines people's understanding of themselves, of their purpose in life and of their relationship to everything else that happens.

There is another way of presenting what is basically the same argument. In Conglomerate Societies there is no machinery, and there are no institutions, through which we can ask and try to answer the three basic community questions which are:

> What are our resources?
> What are our immediate and more distant needs?
> How do we deploy our resources so as to meet our needs in a coherent order of priority?

In societies structured like ours, the only economic question which can be discussed and decided by governments and legislators is:

> How shall we arrange the *financial* aspects of our affairs in the hope that the decision-takers in the Corporations and the Conglomerates will be *induced* to do some of the things that need doing?

This leaves us with a society which is fundamentally incapable of functioning as a community. It can be nothing more than a collection, or a random heap, of individuals all pursuing their own purposes with whatever resources they may have. But does this matter? The answer will depend largely on whether we are Individualists or Wholists. Individualists — and particularly the luckiest and the most powerful of them — will be able to pursue their individual aims just as well, and probably in many ways rather better, in a society which cannot function as a community. To Individualists — provided, of course, that the masses behave properly — the functioning of the Whole is relatively unimportant. At best it is little more than the arena within which they promote their own individual development. Wholists, by contrast, will be profoundly concerned for the structure of the Whole to which they would make their tiny contributions in their freely chosen ways. They will surely hope that they — or, maybe, their descendants — will one day live in a society that is so structured that it can function as a coherent community.

I am making it clear that the establishment of the Common Ownership Community is something that must lie at least half a century ahead of us, and perhaps a good deal more. It depends on there being a massive change in understanding, as well as developments in the world situation some of which can be dimly foreseen. People are wildly unrealistic if they suppose that a transformation of this magnitude can be bashed through in one or two Parliaments by anything so feeble as a rather chancy majority in the House of Commons. The grip of powerful Individualists on all the effective levers of power is far too strong to allow for any such shallow hope. But this does not mean that for the time being the issue is so irrelevant as to deserve no consideration. The quasi-conspiratorial activities of Militant are understandable, and perhaps even justifiable, when the entire company of conventionally respectable people seem unanimous for the unending persistence of Conglomerate Society. As I see it, few things could so quickly reduce the increasing bloody-mindedness of our society as the manifest emergence of a significant and steadily growing company of intelligent and well informed people firmly insisting that, in due course, the Common Ownership Community is our sure destiny.

Meanwhile there is an important question about the ways in which Wholists should live their lives in a society whose structure will still be determined by Individualists for many years. This is not an unprecedented question. Through the sixth to the ninth centuries, Christians had to decide how to live their lives in societies known to be exposed to the inroads of the next wave of marauding barbarians. For sure, if people agree with the argument that has been offered, they will want to persuade others to share their agreement. But life cannot depend only on what people say and write. Far more important is what they do. I believe that from hour to hour and from month to month all Wholists should exert themselves, in whatever area their influence can reach, *to make the Individualists' society run as 'un-badly' as possible.*

Except perhaps for those who work in one of the caring professions — probation officers, teachers, nurses and the like — Wholists ought not to confine themselves to the care of their own families and to the work from which they earn their money. How are children and adolescents to grow up with any real sense of social responsibility if they never see or hear their parents engaging in any kind of cooperative activity that could make the life of their immediate neighbourhood a little more friendly and enjoyable than it would otherwise be? Of course it is wrong to shuffle off social obligations onto charity so as to save money for rich and middling tax payers. But the opposite extreme can be just as bad. Tax payers' money can buy warmth for lonely old people in cold weather; but it cannot buy personal friendship or a sense of there being someone who cares. Local enterprises needing personal cooperation are so many, so various and so easily found by those who want to find them, that there is no need to make a list. Wholists can look around and freely decide where they can be most happily useful. But in these days it needs to be said that the local work is not now confined to what could have been traditionally described as 'charitable' — not confined, that is to say, to those with time and money generously expending themselves to help others who are in need. There is a new spirit abroad, and increasingly people come together locally so as to 'do their own thing' for the sake of a more creative and sustainable life style. These local enterprises can be seen as living green shoots coming up through cracks in the concrete of a psychologically sick and disintegrating society. The majority of those who participate in the innumerable different aspects of this local work probably have not described themselves either as Holists or as Wholists. I hope that many will recognise themselves as such when the word, and its significance, are put to them.

In the work for which they earn their money, Wholists will be conspicuous for the fact that they will always 'go the extra mile'[4]. More explicitly, they will always exert themselves diligently and creatively to promote the success of whatever they are doing, and will behave so as to spread an atmosphere of enthusiasm and cooperation *and honest hard work* as far as their influence can reach. Although many Wholists will see that a Corporationalised Society

[4] Matthew 5.41.

perpetuates mass unemployment, yet, in the immediate situation, efficient and profitable enterprises, moved by good personal relations, are likely to employ more people than those that are permeated by ill will and teetering on the brink of bankruptcy. For such reasons as these, Wholists should always do their utmost, in every possible way, to promote the good success of the enterprise in which they work.

It seems unquestionable that the argument of the last three paragraphs has been correct from a religious standpoint. But many of those who work on the Left, and particularly those of them who tend towards Militant, would rejoice in their confident atheism and would despise anything that claims religious support. This is a sad part of our inheritance from Karl Marx who, despite his many penetrating new thoughts and concepts, never considered the possibility that the answer to a wrong religion ought to be a better religion. Some of today's bishops do well, and particularly many of the Roman Catholics in South America, in knowing that Christianity has to be on the side of the poor. But because of the prevailing agnosticism and atheism on the British Left, I would commend my argument at the rather lower level of long term political strategy. In almost incredulous contempt, members of Militant, who join me in disliking to-day's money-grubbing society, would ask if it can possibly make sense that we should all exert ourselves, wherever our personal influence can reach, to help the existing order of society to endure. They have forgotten that the present order, based on the need to sustain everlasting increase in material production and consumption, cannot endure for another 150 years and may collapse sooner. This certainty will be discussed in the next chapter. When collapse looms more obviously, shall those who will then still love the present system say: 'This system worked well in the past, and it would work now if you Commies weren't out to ditch it'? Or shall we put ourselves in a position from which we can say: 'We told you that it couldn't work; and although you saw us always doing our best to make it work, you now see that it won't'?[5]

One thing more. Within their own ideology, Individualists may have a point when they plug their line that Common Ownership 'means' Dictatorship. There might well be elements of truth in this if society were still to be dominated by Individualists. The possibilities could be quite different when very large numbers deeply know themselves to be Wholists. Our ancestors, in the last thousand years or so, have been in this sort of place before. Medieval society, in its early creative centuries, could never have been run by men who shared the outlook of Hengist and Horsa. Individualist society, all through its outburst of industrial and political innovation, could not have been run by the sort of men who, perhaps rather conveniently, killed so many of each other during the Wars of the Roses. With this in mind, I may be right in thinking that those who know themselves to be Wholists should exert themselves, in every possible way, to increase the number of those who share their basic faith. This, surely, they will best do if they *behave as Wholists* in every possible way within whatever part of society their influence can reach; and this even though, for quite a long time, our whole society will still be dominated by the overwhelmingly powerful Individualists.

[5] I worked out the practical argument for this strategy at chapter length in a self-published book produced in 1974. It can now be had only by writing to *The Next Step*, College, Broadclyst, Exeter, enclosing £1 and self-addressed envelope to carry a normal paperback and stamped for 150 gms.

8

The Way of Evolution

If a dawning reverence for evolution will be, for many of our contemporaries, their first step in a religious direction, then we ought to attend to an almost childlike question: Where is evolution trying to go? Only in this century has it been understood that the course of evolution has to some extent come under the control of our collective decisions. For sure, we cannot precisely forecast what is to happen. But, to the best of our abilities, we ought to look far down the dimly lighted pathway of the future so as to ask about evolution's probable general direction.

When writing in the early 1970s, it seemed to need quite a long argument to show that the course of evolution cannot be represented by any kind of smooth line. By the late 1980s there seems to be a general consensus that it is better pictured as a shallow stairway with immensely long treads linked to each other by rare and relatively sudden risers when the process makes a break-through from one level to the next. At each of these we can ask what was achieved? And this is best answered by looking back to see the limitation of the earlier period that had to be transcended, or the lack that needed to be made good. For example, before the first of the great climacterics there was no life on earth. All sorts of exciting things were happening, such as thunderstorms and earthquakes; but there was no possibility for any plant or animal. Then came living cells, and life set about developing in the waters. But that was the limitation! It was transcended in three further dramatic changes when first the plants, then the insects and then the amphibians came out of the water so as to live on land in air. Plants and animals then developed in profusion, but for a long age animals depended on innumerable kinds of egg-layers. There seems to have been another evolutionary transformation when the mammals bore their babies alive, and then suckled them, from the bodies of their females. Amongst the mammals, for millions of years, none had anything that could be described as self-consciousness, nor could any express their thoughts in words. These limitations were transcended when our kind of creatures came along.

The people who first moved down to cultivate the alluvial valleys were not conscious of being involved in a rare evolutionary break-through. But they were. Their work enabled and (if only for the sake of flood control) required far more extensive social organisation than ever before. The earlier little wandering tribes had slowly improved their tools and had even learned to scatter seed on prepared ground for later harvesting. But in no way could they sustain anything describable as civilisation. The change from civilisation impossible to civilisation possible seems to be an evolutionary event comparable to the change from the impossibility, to the possibility, of life on land in air.

From the earliest civilisations until almost our own times, all large civilisations have been authoritarian; all have been overwhelmingly agricultural; all, with very modest contributions from the streams and the winds, have been muscle-driven. Now, within the last few centuries, we begin to see the struggling emergence of a new evolutionary development of the first magnitude. It was triggered by two major events. One of these was the outbreak of Democracy — of the fierce demand from ever increasing numbers of people that they should participate in the management of their lives. Democracy can be suppressed over large areas and perhaps for long times; but it is now endemic in our world and, no matter through what suffering, it will never be destroyed. The other and interlocking development was the Industrial Revolution. Through these two great changes, evolution is making another of its rare and astonishing advances.

What were these two irreversible and once-and-once-only developments really meant to do? This question, as with every other evolutionary break-through, is best answered by looking at the terrible lack which had dominated the earlier situation — the profound limitation that needed to be overcome.

All the earlier civilisations were *Necessarily Divided Societies*. By the fact of their being muscle-driven, they were inevitably divided into two quite different kinds of people living their lives by two quite different sets of rules. There were the Uppers who could enjoy all the possibilities of civilised experimentation because they were sustained by far larger numbers of Lowers who lived sometimes just above, sometimes on and often well below the conditions that we now arrange for our farmyard animals. Varying numbers of Middlings do not affect the basic truth; they served the Uppers and depended on the Lowers.

As lately as in 1853, John Creech, in search of work, walked twenty-five miles from my great great grandfather's estate near Porlock to my great great uncle's estate near Tiverton. Finding none, he walked twenty-four of the miles back before dying in the snow on Dunkery Beacon. Next day his widow came begging and the vicar gave her a shilling.[1] Meanwhile my ancestors were enjoying every comfort and, according to their choice, could afford any of the luxuries that the situation then allowed. The decisive point is that at the time almost no one saw anything wrong with it. This did not in any way depend on the social wickedness of the Uppers. Just as life on earth, for example, had been locked through a long age at the level of the cold-blooded egg-layers, so, through millennia, it was locked at the level of the Necessarily Divided Societies where there could have been no civilisation at all unless the people had been divided into the two different kinds living under two entirely different sets of rules.

The two interlocking and quite recent developments

[1] From the manuscript diary of the Reverend Joshua Stephenson, Rector of Selworthy, near Minehead, from 1802 to 1863; it is now in the Somerset Record Office.

ought to persuade us that we are living in the early stages of a new evolutionary break-through from one level of life to the next. Out ahead of us we can dimly discern what I would now call the Wholist Civilisations of the future. In these civilisations, all will live under the same basic rules, all will be equally valued despite their widely differing abilities and all will be equally concerned to promote the social good health of the community in which they live. It is absurd to speculate about details, but I should hope that the spread of income from richest to poorest would be less than five to one.

It is obvious that we have already moved a good way from the Necessarily Divided Societies of the past and towards the Wholist Civilisations of the future. This is to be expected because it would be unlikely that the two great forces making for evolutionary development could start working in the world more than two hundred years ago without yet producing any effect whatever. It is equally obvious that, both materially and spiritually, Wholist Civilisations are a long way ahead of us. For at least three obdurate reasons, it is unlikely that these future civilisations will ever be fully established except on the yonder side of incalculable strife and suffering. For anyone to expect anything other would be contrary to the evolutionary experience of the earth.

Even during its long relatively level periods, when no astonishing changes were in course, evolution has depended on enormous numbers of creatures being killed and eaten by others. We shall never know exactly what happened at the rare moments of break-through from one level to the next, because there is no way in which we can now go back and look. But, if part of today's speculation is anywhere near the mark, how many billions of some kind of lung-fish must have gasped out their dying breaths in desiccating puddles before, at last, life found out how to live on land in air? If suffering is a universal rule of development, we may better understand what Teilhard de Chardin had in mind when he suggested that Jesus 'will become more and more in the eyes of believers "he who bears and supports the weight of the world in evolution".' Of this possibility he wrote:

> The meaning of the Cross is taking on greater breadth and dynamism for us: the Cross which is now the symbol not merely of the dark retrogressive side of the universe in genesis, but also and, even more, of its triumphant and luminous side; the Cross which is the symbol of progress and victory won through mistakes, disappointments and hard work; the only Cross, in very truth, that we can honestly, proudly and passionately offer for the worship of a world which has become conscious of what it was yesterday and what awaits it tomorrow.[2]

The first cause for almost incalculable strife and suffering during the next few generations comes from the exponential growth of the planet's population. We do not yet know what maximum number of people can be sustained in basic decency in power-and-technology-driven civilisations. But populations cannot expand at anything like the rate that we have known during this century without global disaster. It is utterly true that populations cannot be limited simply by the universal availability of cheap mechanical or chemical contraceptives; but it is equally certain that disastrous population explosion cannot be avoided without them. It is also true that population expansion has not been caused by educated Roman Catholics obeying their Popes. Indeed, as Bishop Montefiore wrote, in advanced countries the comparative family sizes amongst people of different faiths show that the reiterated demand 'seems to be falling on ears which, if not deaf, at least are hard of hearing.'[3] But this is a relatively trivial fact in the face of impending disaster. Throughout the whole of this century,

[2] *Christianity and Evolution* (Collins, 1971) p. 163.
[3] *Doom or Deliverance* (Manchester University Press, 1972) p.9.

a really sustained and hugely financed global determination to hold down the exponential growth of the world's population has been aborted by the morally unjustifiable attitude of one of the most politically powerful institutions on earth. *Morally* unjustifiable? Yes; I think so. Moral theologians and philosophers have almost unanimously agreed that when we consider sin and evil it is always the intention that decisively counts; the exact method of its execution is almost irrelevant. Can anyone justify the proposition that it is quite all right for married couples to intend the joys of sexual intercourse without (or without further) childbearing, provided that they put their intention into practice by one or other of two methods which are both unreliable?

I very much hope that I am wrong. But I fear that our planet has passed the point of no return on the way to global famine on a scale far exceeding anything that we have experienced up to now; and that, when it happens, even almost inconceivable generosity from the rich to the poor will be far too little to prevent the starving from dying, not in tens, but in hundreds of millions.

The second reason for expecting early and widespread distress comes from what was offered in 1954 through *The Challenge of Man's Future.*[4] It will be remembered that Harrison Brown tried to warn us that we ought to prepare seriously for a not distant future when we shall have to stop living on the planet's capital and learn to live on its annual income. Confronted with this challenge, most people respond with: 'Give me the facts and then I'll take it seriously'. For most intelligent and reasonably well informed people this is almost wholly untrue. Very few of them can now honestly say that the essential facts have not already been drawn to their attention. And then, 'Orig-

[4] See p. 6 above.

inal Sin' either prevented them from considering the facts or, if they actually looked at them, made them soon forget what they momentarily knew.[5]

Brown's book was greeted with almost total public silence which lasted into the 1970s. Since then, small minorities of concerned and well disposed people have made all the basic facts available to anyone emotionally capable of looking at them and holding them in mind. An incomplete list would be *The Limits to Growth*,[6] *Blueprint for Survival*,[7] *Global 2000*,[8] *North-South*[9] and *Our Common Future*[10]. I was particularly impressed by Willy Brandt in *North-South* and by Gro Brundtland in *Our Common Future*. Brandt: 'It is not just a risk to the environment, it is a plundering of our planet, without regard to the generations to come.' Brundtland: 'We borrow environmental capital from future generations with no intention or prospect of repaying . . . because we can get away with it: future generations do not vote.'[11] Though the words were far less widely publicised, I was also moved by Professor Dennis Gabor: 'Either steer society into a state of zero economic growth, or else face an overshoot, followed by a collapse of our industrial civilisation . . . We must detach hope from economic growth.' And by Charles Luce: 'If we are to preserve a habitable earth we must be willing to accept fewer goods and services, including less electricity.'[12] Gabor was a Nobel Prize Physicist; but

[5] See pp. 42–5.

[6] A report for the Club of Rome by Dennis Meadows and others at the Massachusetts Institute of Technology, published in Britain by Earth Island Press in March 1972.

[7] A single-subject issue of the *Ecologist* for January, 1972.

[8] Produced by the State Department and other organisations in Washington and published in Britain as a Penguin Original in 1982.

[9] Produced by an Independent Commission under Willy Brandt and published in Britain by Pan Books in 1980.

[10] Produced by the World Commission on Environment under Gro Brundtland and published by OUP in 1987.

[11] Brandt, *Op. cit:* p.20; Brundtland, p.8.

[12] Gabor in a lecture to Malvern School sixth form in 1973 of which I obtained a verbatim copy; Luce in *International Digest*, January 1973, p.76.

perhaps Luce was more impressive because he was chairman of ConEd which probably produces and sells more electricity than any other corporation in the world; and one would expect that his professional self-interest would prevent him from seeing the truth.

The consequences of our collective profligacy will begin to produce their serious effects well before the end of the twenty-first century. So do we look at babies snoozing in their cots or kicking on the floor — many of us looking at our own children, grandchildren or great grandchildren — and do we give them 'Damn you, Jack, I'm all right'? Surprising as it may seem to some of today's church-goers, this is a religious question. For most of those who are quite intelligent enough to know the facts, the appalling truth is that we do.

I have already described how my Bevanite colleagues were emotionally prevented from admitting Harrison Brown's facts into their conscious minds.[13] Other and opposite, but far stronger, emotional forces are at work in the depths of Individualists, and particularly in those of them who are absorbed in Party Politics. The whole political philosophy of Individualists depends on faith. It depends on the faith that there can be and will be and, far more important, that *there simply must be* steady persistent and exponential growth in the annual production and consumption of material goods extending indefinitely into the future.

Sir Keith Joseph, now retired from the struggle, was at one time the high priest of this religion. In 1975 he sponsored a pamphlet produced by the Centre for Policy Studies and titled *Why Britain Needs a Social Market Economy.*[14] In it we were told:

> By encouraging the energies and initiative of the creative and sturdier members of one society, the resources avail-

[13] See p. 6 above.
[14] The CPS was founded jointly by Sir Keith and Margaret Thatcher in 1974.

> able for helping the aged, the sick and the disabled are substantially enlarged.[15]

Quite modest research would find scores of public statements from political Individualists making the same general point. You encourage the sturdy and ambitious, and at the same time the slick and the pushful, by allowing them more money; this is the best way of enlarging the total material cake; so in the end the least fortunate will have rather bigger slices. It is the only moral justification for the Individualists' political philosophy. If the planet imposes firm veto on everlasting exponential growth in the total material cake, and still more if it challenges us to learn to live on a smaller material cake in a not very distant future, the whole of the Individualists' political philosophy collapses. When facts conflict with the ideology of people's Political Party, it is almost certainty that the facts will be emotionally ignored so that the ideology can be sustained.

Only very few Wholists are likely to be saints. The rest naturally appreciate the comforts and even the luxuries that come their way. But these do not constitute the purpose and the hope of their lives. For this reason, Wholists would gladly make their material contribution to the very large public expenditure that would now be needed if we deliberately set out to equip our community with all the social capital that our grandchildren and great grandchildren will need if they are not to face 'a collapse in our industrial civilisation' when they are suddenly forced to live on the planet's income. If our society had an effective majority of Wholists, the necessary work and cost would supply 'something with which we can dispense no longer: a deliberate and avowed moral purpose, involving the call for common sacrifice for a recognised common good.'[16]

Even those Wholists who are now quite rich, or at least very comfortable, would far prefer to live in private

[15] *Op. cit:* p.7.
[16] See p. 4 above.

modesty amidst public worth than in the private affluence amidst public squalour that is imposed on us by our contemporary Individualism. They would be able to 'detach hope from economic growth' and could accept an almost inevitable decrease in annual material consumption because, as Dennis Meadows wrote:

> Any human activity that does not require a large flow of irreplaceable resources or produce severe environmental degradation might continue to grow indefinitely. In particular, those pursuits that many people would list as the most desirable and satisfying activities of man — education, art, music, religion, basic scientific research, athletics and social interactions — could flourish.[17]

Members of small minorities with the guts to recognise the planetary challenge, have recently formed courageous and valuable organisations such as Greenpeace, Friends of the Earth and the Green Party. If many of these people have not yet consciously felt themselves to be religious in the conventional sense of the word, I hope they will consider whether Wholism is the all-embracing description of their attitude to life. I think too that they should hope rather less from the effort to bash the facts into the Individualists' brains, and should attend rather more to the possibility of converting them from Individualism to Wholism. For sure they should persist with immediate campaigns where the prospect of early modest success seems hopeful. The two tasks can go on at the same time, thus recalling one of the most glorious episodes in the history of the Church when, 'as it struggled with the surrounding barbarism, the work of conversion and of social reconstruction had been almost indistinguishable.'[18]

The third obdurate reason for expecting inestimable

[17] In *Limits to Growth* p. 175.
[18] See p. 18 above.

further suffering was clearly stated by the UN Experts who tried to show what would be needed to turn President Truman's 'Point Four' from hope into reality. They wrote:

> In our judgment there are a number of under-developed countries where the concentration of economic wealth and political power in the hands of a small class, whose main interest is the preservation of their own wealth and privilege, rules out the prospect of much economic progress until a social revolution has affected a shift in the distribution of income and power.[19]

In the middle 1980s, this fact seems to have been well understood by the people in Managua where — without by any means 'nationalising' everything in sight — they cared more for the health and education of the people than for the freedoms of big landowners and multi-national corporations.[20] In Washington they could see it all only as the expansion of an 'evil Empire' into their back yard. At the time of my writing, the outcome of the local disagreement is uncertain. But, on a world scale, the problem highlighted by the UN experts is bound to involve further suffering and strife.

If the full establishment of Wholist Civilisations lies so far ahead of us, and through so much future suffering, is there any point in thinking about it now? I think there is. However arduous the journey, a general understanding of the destination gives us a sense of direction which can be useful in the decisions that have to be made from week to week and from year to year. For sure, we have amongst us large numbers of people who quite naturally feel that civilised societies always have been divided into two different kinds living by two different sets of rules, and that this is therefore the way things will always be. But fishes, if they had been able to think, might have supposed that life must always be confined to the waters. Whenever

[19] *Op. cit:* pp. 15–16; See footnote on p. 5 above.

[20] See, amongst many other possible sources, *Nicaragua: The Threat of a Good Example*, by Diana Melrose (Oxfam, 1985).

an unprecedented evolutionary development becomes possible, it simultaneously becomes evolutionarily necessary; and those who strive against it will be leading to disaster.

9

Towards the Transcendent

An important and quite recent change in the religious outlook of our contemporaries has been mentioned more than once. In earlier times very large numbers of people found little difficulty in accepting the transcendent Truth — accepting, that is to say, the presence and the companionship of God, either 'Up There' or 'Out There'. Many church-goers must have lived on quite good terms with this external Divinity without — or without often — knowing about the Truth within. It was correct to say that in most of us this pattern has recently been reversed. It is now easier — or at any rate less difficult — to begin to know the Truth in our own depths than to become aware of any Ultimate Reality living and working outside of ourselves. It will be recalled that in the early 1960s the then Archbishop of Canterbury knew that he would make contact with an Oxford audience more directly if he assured them that he would start 'from what is already going on inside you'.

Many people in our day will first be open to transcendent Truth through particular and unusual experiences. To most of them it seems that these experiences are not offered very often. To put the matter anthropomorphically, it is as if God were saying: 'I showed you once (or twice) and that ought to be enough'. I am moved to quote an account of one such experience written by my mother as part of the story of her childhood:

'On a bland spring day, Milly had flung herself down on a sunny bank under the wall of the wood, just to bask, as every other living thing was basking, in the warmth

of the May afternoon. We had been out by ourselves gathering primroses — rather uncommon flowers in our countryside, but we had found them in plenty in the places we remembered from last year. There was nothing going on in Milly's head as she let her eyes rove here and there, and saw the oaks in their light dressing of golden-bronze, the ash-trees still obdurately gaunt, the nimble lambs and their muffled up old mothers, the fields and grey walls, and the path winding up past the stables to her home on the hillside. All at once, quite without prelude, an astonishing radiance welled up on all these familiar things and in the child herself. They were no longer just themselves, separate objects with edges of their own; they were that radiance, and the radiance was unbounded, glorious love. Often Milly had said to herself, in vexed perplexity, confronted with the Deity of the church and the little pious books: "I wish, oh, I wish, I could actually see God, just for one minute, then perhaps I would understand." Now, quite clearly and unforgettably, without haste or surprise, she said: "Why, I am seeing God — I could be seeing Him all the time! I am seeing right into God. He is seeing right into me." Even the little girl Milly was aware that this in-seeing cannot last as an incident of time. For once, a prayer of her very own, not quick with fear, broke out in her heart: "Please God, don't let me forget." And she knew that the answer was as real as the prayer; that, even if this in-seeing should never be hers again, the remembrance of it would belong to her for ever.

'It was over already. The world of things around her was dulling back into its ordinary this-and-that. The other two children were calling to her: "Tea, tea! Come on Milly, or we'll be late for tea." Milly scrambled to her feet, picked up her basket of primroses, and resumed her nursery existence.'[1]

[1] *Goodbye for the Present* (Hodder and Stoughton, 1935) pp. 162–3. Her name was Eleanor Cropper; for the sake of better objectivity, she called herself 'Milly' in the book.

Most people seem to suppose that sharp experiences of this kind are offered only to very few, and that there must be something almost freakish about those who receive and recognise them. The truth seems to be very different. In an article in the *Guardian*, David Hay, Director of the Alister Hardy Research Centre, reported some 50 to 60 per cent of our people as saying that at least once or twice in their lives they have had some kind of religious experience — an awareness of the presence of God or of a meaningful patterning of their lives which seemed to come from a transcendent source.[2]

Then why do most of us — including most of the recipients — suppose that experiences of this kind come only to rare and rather peculiar people? I believe that the widespread misapprehension is partly caused by the behaviour of a small company of passionate evangelisers. In support of this possibility, I would quote a paragraph which I wrote a quarter of a century ago.

> *Some people are prevented from even holding themselves open towards the possibility of such experience, by the widespread impression that it is virtually reserved for monks and cranks. In a way it is natural. Such an experience is remarkable; and of those to whom it is given, a small proportion cannot help feeling that 'MY' experience must be conclusively convincing to 'YOU'. This, of course, is rubbish; but it does not prevent these people from racing around telling everyone about it and commanding them to join the saved. They are written off as religious cranks; and others — outwardly perhaps rather more normal men and women — maintain embarrassed silence. I think these others are wrong. Their collective silence reinforces the widespread impression that only the abnormal can expect this kind of thing.*[3]

[2] The Research Centre was formerly the Religious Experience Research Unit, founded by Alister Hardy in 1969 and renamed in his honour after his death in 1985. The *Guardian* article was published on July 20th 1987.

[3] *We Teach Them Wrong* (Gollancz, 1963) p. 173.

David Hay confirms that the behaviour of the aggressive evangelisers may be part of the cause for our widespread ignorance of what is actually happening to so many people; I am grateful to him and to the editor of the *Guardian* for permission to quote extensively from his writing.

> *The great majority of people reporting experiences are quite clearly not stupid, weird, or out of touch with everyday reality. On the contrary, experiencers on the whole are better balanced, happier and better educated than people who don't claim religious experience . . . What appears to have happened though, is that as a nation we are taken in by a pervasive negative stereotype. Possibly this is because a minority of people with odd religious obsessions are quite noisy about them, or it may be a more deep seated intuition that belief in the transcendent runs counter to the intellectual tradition which is currently dominant . . . It reminds me of a comment occasionally made by historians, to the effect that cultures despise those aspects of reality which threaten their major preoccupations. I wonder if that has any connection with what to me is the most interesting association uncovered by recent research. With great regularity, people tie in their experience with an alteration in their ethical attitudes and behaviour . . . The experience seems to involve a direct, you could say experimental, discovery that at a deep level we are not isolated from each other or the rest of reality. The psychological distance between the individual and everything else virtually disappears. Even though the gap returns afterwards, the conviction remains that what happened was a revelation of the true state of affairs.*
>
> *The commonplace perception that we are alienated carcasses, meeting and interacting externally and by accident is literally discovered to be a misperception. Monastic mystics might express it as the discovery that all things are One, and very occasionally people put it that way. Usually in this country it is expressed by saying*

> *that we are all part of a single creation, or the children of one God.*
>
> *For people who have entered this experience, ethics is not reducible to a social construction. There is a pragmatic basis for morality; we literally are part of everybody and everything, so care for other people and the environment tends to become an imperative need.*

I hope that I am not being moved by 'something wrong about me as I naturally stand' if I read David Hay as telling us that, in these experiences of contact with the transcendent, people learn that they are not Individualists and discover (even if they do not actually use the word) that they are Wholists.

The Alister Hardy Research Centre can be contacted at Manchester College, 29 George Street, Oxford OX1 2BR. Of the Centre's many publications *Exploring Inner Space* (Pelican 1982, second edition Mowbrays, 1987) is perhaps the best introduction to their whole work.

It would be a mistake to suppose that in these days there can be no move towards the transcendent except through such experiences as have been described by the many people of whom David Hay was writing. There would be a kind of spiritual blackmail in the behaviour of anyone who looked at the God-shaped blank on the inside and said: 'I don't believe in you; but give me a special experience and then perhaps I'll change my mind.' Indeed, it may well be that special experiences will hardly ever break in except on people who are already, in some small way, concerned and open towards them. Are there any means by which anyone can promote this concern or help others to be open to the transcendental possibility? Millions of words in thousands of sermons and in hundreds of books have been directed towards this end; and for those whose minds are still shaped so as to receive them, there is nothing wrong with the words. They express the Truth in one of the ways in which it can properly be expressed. The trouble with these conventional words is precisely that they have become conventionalised. By semi-conscious association, they conjure up the whole 'Message' that now seems to be coming from the Church. Most people feel that they have heard it all before, that they were not much impressed and that they are not likely to be impressed if they hear it all again. Is there any way of expressing the same truth in words that may seem to be fresh and alive today? I should not have been able to find any satisfying answer to this question. In other people's writings, I have been impressed by two passages; one is quite short, the second considerably longer. Other people may not respond to them as positively as I did. I offer them for what they may be worth.

Unexpectedly the shorter passage was written in the very earliest years of our century. It will be recalled that William James forestalled the psychologists of our day in the first part of the 'uniform deliverance in which religions all appear to meet.' It was, he said, a sense of there being 'something wrong about us as we naturally stand.' He said, of those of us who accept the superficially unattractive truth, that 'so far as we suffer from our wrongness and criticise it, we are to that extent consciously beyond it.' It follows that 'along with the wrong part, there is thus a better part of us, even though it may be a most helpless germ.' This can lead to the second part of the common deliverance of all the religions:

> *We become aware that this higher part is conterminous and continuous with a MORE of the same quality, which is operative in the universe outside of us.*[4]

Mysteriously, if we try to serve and cooperate, and not

[4] *Op. cit:* p. 508; see footnote p. 42 above. I have deliberately distorted James by translating from the singular to the plural, thus allowing 'we' and 'us' instead of 'he' and 'him' which were acceptable writing in 1901.

to manipulate, the MORE can afford us direction and strength.

The same basic truth was offered at greater length in a letter from P.W. Martin with whom, as I have said already, I used to have all-day discussions.[5] In one of these, in May 1965, I asked a question to which he gave a very strong answer in about five sentences. Next day I found that I could recall only the general sense of his answer, but nothing like his actual words — nothing, in effect, that I could hand on hopefully to the R.E. students in one of my educational seminar groups. I wrote to Martin, reminding him of the situation in which I asked my question, and wondering whether he could generously recall his answer. It will be clear from a part of his letter that we had been discussing the passage quoted above from William James. Martin wrote:

> *'I don't know that I can put into a couple of paragraphs the gist of what we were talking about when we met. But I can certainly set down — in a rather long letter — what I wish to Heaven someone could have told me years ago, at school, as to the nature of things scientific and religious and what one can do about them. It amounts to this.*
>
> *'If we look squarely at the dark backward of time, it is fairly evident that two processes have been going on, side by side, over the millions of years. There is, on the one hand, the repetitive process, the unchanging "laws" of Nature; the basis on which science, as we know it, consistently works. These "laws" of nature can be relied upon. Hydrogen, to the best of our knowledge, always has behaved and always will behave as hydrogen. We may get to know more about it as time goes on; but, in common with the rest of the repetitive process, hydrogen has its own way of acting and blessedly sticks to it.*
>
> *'Along with this repetitive process there is an innovating activity; wholly new entities come into existence;*

[5] See p. 10 above.

things that have never been there before. The first manifest sign of this innovative activity here on earth is that, some two thousand million years back, there came life. Before, over the hundreds of millions of years since the planet took shape, there had been a lifeless world. Then came the "intertidal scum" or whatever it may have been; living matter; something utterly different in kind from anything previously existent here on earth.

'Over the next many millions of years, this was followed by other extraordinary manifestations of the innovating activity. Some strange organising, whole-making capacity resulted in the emergence of countless millions of individual creatures, ranging all the way from dinosaurs to the cholera germ. It is as if, from the first coming of life, a continuous experimenting has been going forward, on a gigantic scale.

'This manifold emergence of self-moving individuals, each variously working out its own experiment in living, led on to the next great creative leap, the coming into existence of consciousness. Living individual creatures became directly aware of their environment, by way of their senses, with one particular type of creature — man — becoming directly aware of himself; asking such questions as: What am I? What is it all about?

'Then, in the course of relatively recent times, has come the strangest innovation of all: the passion for rightness which is the distinguishing mark of man, rightness even if it is aginst one's own personal self-interest. And, with this passion for rightness, there have emerged the great values, the great impulses stirring in us, the very essence, as we feel, of the true greatness of man: undemanding love; the devoted search for truth; the urge to wholeness, including that special kind of wholeness we call beauty; the urge to create.

'The branch of knowledge — of wisdom — directly concerned with the innovating activity is religion. But here, pitifully, we are still putting things out in a way that may have been appropriate eight hundred years ago, but is murder today. No modern youngster worthy of his

salt is going to take somebody's say-so about God, on the grounds that he ought to believe it and that it is all for his own good.

'What we should be saying, as I see it — what somebody at school could have said to me, but did not — is something like this. As a scientific fact of life there are these two activities at work. Learning to work with the repetitive process can be immensely valuable provided we put what we learn there to good use. At present, though, we are putting it to very mixed use. In our lifetime it may well be mis-employed to wipe us all out.

'The key question is: how can we put it to good use? And this is where the innovating activity comes in. By far the greatest of all the discoveries ever come upon is that man is able to make direct contact with a creative process at work in life. This creative process, as it were, takes over exactly at the point which the long-term innovative process has brought us to — the passion for rightness; the great values — love, truth, wholeness, beauty, the creative urge. By making direct contact with the creative process, these immense possibilities of life can be enabled to operate more effectively. In this way, life can be utterly changed — one's own life and the life of the world.

'How anyone personally sets about making contact with the creative process is for each of us to find out in his or her own way. No one can do it for us. But the means by which it is done are reasonably well known. There are three main approaches, all of them essential, each keying in with the other two. Which of these approaches we hit on first is a matter of how life comes to us. But everyone needs to be on the look out for the lot.

'Most immediate of all is the creative change that takes place inside oneself. We are all born, and grow up through childhood, with a "me" attitude to most things; me in the middle; me first; me all the time. A world made up of me-in-the-middle people would be a jungle. Happily it is possible to get beyond this merely savage and infantile stage. In all of us there is a deeper centre, a different basis of being, a true self as against the me-in-the-middle self. By going down into one's very depths one comes upon this true self — the Godhead immanent in theological terms. Insofar as we learn to live from this deep centre, instead of the me-in-the-middle, we truly become people and are able to serve life to the full.

'Along with this finding of the real self, there is a further potentiality to which the real self gives access. Provided we are living from the deep centre we can, as it were, draw upon the creative source itself — the MORE as it has been called: for strength; for help; for courage; for endurance; for all those things needed when life gets too difficult, when we are up against something that could easily get us down if we did not have this reinforcement. One has to learn from experience how the creative contact can be made. No one can simply switch it on. But the possibility is there, unfailingly, for all those who learn to live from the depths of their utmost being and turn to the MORE.

'The third means of approach to the creative process is the closest, the least known and in many ways the most valuable of all. Expressed in simple, primitive language, it is that there is a "Companion" that goes along with us, a Helper, a Friend, a Counsellor, a Co-worker, who in many ways sees much more clearly than we can what is our right course. By making contact with this Counsellor and Co-worker we can get things done to an extent and on a scale utterly impossible to us in the ordinary way.

'Most decent people, so far as one can gather, both know and don't know of this "informing spirit". They are likely to come upon it from time to time but usually do not know what it is that they are experiencing; and more or less make a mess of it. Even when I was at school, I was dimly aware that if I did something because, in some funny fashion, it was "right" (as distinct from the hundred-and-one me-in-the-middle reasons) things went quite differently. Problems worked themselves out. Words came to my mind I had never consciously thought of — the right words. In all sorts of ways, I was being helped. But it usually ended up with my thinking it was all my own clever doing; and at once it fell down. No one ever put me straight as to what it was all about.

'And there was nothing I needed to know more. The man who is unaware of this possibility of the informing spirit, has not even begun to pull his weight in the world. There are conditions, of course. What we are trying to do has to be in the right direction — the direction of the creative. If and when one starts thinking (as I did) that it is all one's own clever doing; or imagines one can turn it on for one's own purposes; there quickly comes a most infernal mess. But if we are living as best we can from the deep centre, the true self, instead of me-in-the-middle; if we are making the creative contact with the MORE — getting our strength and courage at source; then, with the Counsellor and Co-worker helping, we can be all of twice the man we once were.

'This, of course, is no new doctrine. The creative process, the different spiritual dimension, interpenetrating the repetitive life, is what religion terms the Kingdom of God, the Kingdom of Heaven, the world invisible transforming the space–time world. The going over to the different basis of being from the me-in-the-middle state is the discovery of the "Kingdom of Heaven" within a man. The creative source, the MORE, is the Heavenly Father, the giver of the daily bread by which the true self lives and grows, by which the Kingdom of Heaven comes here on earth. The Counsellor and Co-worker is the Holy Ghost, the Comforter, the Spirit of Truth. It is all there, and much else beside, in the Christian Gospels, but in a form no longer accessible to the present-day boy or girl setting forth in the world. That of course is why education is necessary; the leading out from the meaningless life into the life that has meaning and purpose and fulfilment. That also is why this present age, with its race to catch up with the misuse of the repetitive process, is the most exciting age to be born into, to learn the facts about, and do what we can.'

10

Christianity?

In earlier chapters, the Church's contemporary teaching was so often criticised that some people will suppose that I cannot be any kind of Christian. In fact I believe that Jesus was, and is, the unique manifestation of the ultimate truth about life. I believe it while joining the huge company who must add 'Help thou my unbelief'; while knowing that my attitude might be different if I had been born into a good home, say, in Cairo, Allahabad or Bangkok rather than in London.

I am not forgetting that in these days it may be counter-productive to commend Jesus directly to our secular majority. This chapter is therefore offered to those who now understand the importance of the religious dimension of living, either because they could accept the basic affirmation that was offered, or for some other reason. These people, as I said, will be open to meet Jesus in their own experience; and this means that if they become Christians it will not be because they are told, but because they will find out. If this is true it is quite possible that in a hundred years' time there will be even fewer professing Christians than there are today. This will be alarming for those who claim to care for Christianity while actually being concerned for the maintenance, and if possible the aggrandisement, of their own institutional organisation. But it will be perfectly acceptable to those who are concerned for the long future of the Christian faith. After all, through the early centuries of the Church's childhood, the percentage of the population who were open or secret Christians must have been quite small; so there is nothing to worry about if the same should turn out to be true of the early centuries in the Church's adolescence.

I was very recently impressed by words attributed to Pierre Ceresole (1879–1945) of whom previously I had not been aware. He wrote:

> If you allow me to have Christ as a friend, he may become what you call a God; if you impose him on me as God, he cannot become a friend.[1]

I suppose that such words, two hundred years ago, would have been understood by very few. Today they probably describe the attitude of a majority of our secular people. Then what can be done by a not very devout Christian who would like other people to share his convictions? It could be dangerous to offer 'particular and unusual experiences' because, as I have said already, 'MY' experience cannot be conclusively convincing to 'YOU'.[2]

It might be better, perhaps, to offer some of the thoughts which have linked themselves onto the experiences even while knowing that they cannot establish the same kind of experience in others. And perhaps, following Pierre Ceresole, one could try to write so as to allow Jesus to seem like a possible friend.

The gospel-making process has already been described.[3] The story was carried through several decades by oral tradition — by the mouth-to-ear enthusiasm of the earliest believers. As we saw, this process is sure to produce wonder tales out of nothing. It can never produce insight. It seems, therefore, that we might look at our four Gospels

[1] Quoted by Ormerod Greenwood in *Quaker Monthly*, December 1987, p. 239.

[2] I have nonetheless, tried to describe one of my two critical experiences in *We Teach Them Wrong* (Gollancz 1963), pp. 173–5.

[3] See pp. 50-53 above.

to see if we find insight. For a start, suppose that instead of our four Gospels, we had only the story of the temptations and the parables of the Good Samaritan and of the Prodigal Son.[4] The temptations have been considered already.[5] The two parables have done more than any other stories in human language, the one to make us more careful about others' needs, and the other to make us more generous to ourselves. Those who live without spectacular vice or virtue may not know how many saints and sinners, knowing the enormity of their own failures, might have given up in despair if they had not known the Parable of the Prodigal Son.

Or we can gather some of the other recorded sayings of Jesus. 'Man does not live by bread alone . . . I have not come to call the righteous, but sinners, to repentance . . . But *I* say "Love your enemies. Do good to them that hate you; bless them that curse you; pray for those who treat you spitefully" . . . Pass no judgments and you will not be judged; for as you judge others, so shall you yourselves be judged . . . Why do you look at the speck of sawdust in your brother's eye, with never a thought for the great plank in your own eye? . . . Where your treasure is, there will your heart be also — you cannot serve God and Money . . . The gate that leads to life is small and the road is narrow, and those who find it are few . . . But seek and you shall find, knock and the door will be opened . . . Seek ye first the kingdom of God and his righteousness. Go and learn what the text means: "I require mercy, not sacrifice" . . . Among you, whoever wants to be first must be the willing slave of all . . . What will a man gain by winning the whole world at the cost of his true self? And what can he give that will buy that self back?

'Blessed are the poor in spirit, the meek, the merciful and the pure in heart; blessed the peacemakers and those who share the sorrows of the world; blessed are they who hunger and thirst after righteousness and suffer per-

[4] Luke 10. 30–37 and 15. 11–32.
[5] See p. 51 above.

secution for righteousness' sake. They shall be comforted, strengthened, satisfied; they shall obtain mercy and shall inherit the earth; they shall see God and be called the children of God, for theirs is the kingdom of heaven.

'Father, forgive them; they don't know what they're doing.'[6]

Jesus displays himself, not only in his words, but in the whole course of his life. It is particularly in action that Jesus can seem to surpass the sages of eastern faiths. Some people say, perhaps rightly, that many eastern mystics have penetrated the heart of reality more deeply than any but a few of the saints in the West. But how did these eastern mystics live? Most of them taught a few selected disciples, lived austerely but not uncomfortably in their monasteries and died in old age. Jesus went out to help and teach anyone who would listen. Such was his spectacular death that many good church-goers can read the Gospels without really noticing two lesser episodes: after his only reported sermon, the respectable congregation tried to throw him off a cliff; after his longest recorded question-and-answer session, the same sort of people tried to kill him in a volley of stones.[7]

What did Jesus look like? If we are to 'see' him in action, it would be good to visualise him as he probably was. In a white man's continent, it may have been a pardonable convention for artists to portray the holy family as if they had been Whites. But we may now be at a moment in history when it is important to remember that they were not. Two thousand years ago all the inhabitants of the Middle East were brown — some of them quite dark brown at that. European Whites would never have heard of Jesus unless brown men had travelled by land and sea to tell us.

Apart from colour, many stained glass windows damage

[6] Translations from several sources, mostly the Authorised Version or the New English Bible; the conflation of the Beatitudes (Matthew 5. 3–11) is mine.

[7] Luke 4. 16–30; John 8. 12–59.

us by seeming to support the deadly line about 'gentle Jesus meek and mild'. It would be difficult to find five other words that would make him seem less attractive, say, to the top formers in a typical comprehensive school. Many of the windows that purport to show the crucifixion are particularly misleading; arms rising but gently from the horizontal; elbows slightly bent; the body apparently immune from the force of gravity; all conveying an impression of unreality, as if the thing had never actually happened. If we want a more likely mental image of Jesus as he was seen by his contemporaries, we might picture the kind of man whom eight international forwards would like to have behind them at scrum half.

What sort of people, in action, became the friends and enemies of Jesus? The enemies were outstandingly the hypocrites — respectable leaders of society whose outward self-righteousness covered less acceptable inner qualities. 'Whited sepulchres', he called them, 'which indeed appear beautiful outwardly, but are within full of dead men's bones and all uncleanness.'[8] Today's psychologists say more gently: 'Don't pretend you are better than you are; acknowledge the evil forces in yourself.' The particular friends of Jesus were at the other end of the social spectrum. Again the stained glass windows can mislead us; they suggest that everything was unreal because it was all done in dressing gowns. Even the superb language of the Authorised Version can lull us into a sense of unreality. Without recognising anything of importance we can read:

> And it came to pass, as Jesus sat at meat in the house, behold many publicans and sinners came and sat down with him and his disciples. And when the Pharisees saw it, they said unto his disciples 'Why eateth your master with publicans and sinners?'[9]

But what if we retranslate it?

[8] Matthew 23. 27.
[9] Matthew 9. 10–11.

> And it so happened that as Jesus was eating in the house a whole gang of yobs, tarts and quislings swarmed in and joined the party. A group of school governors who saw it asked his followers 'Why does he mix with all that riff-raff?'

Not only did Jesus enjoy the riff-raff; but they seem to have enjoyed him. Our psychologists say: 'Get to know yourself better. "Sit down at meat" with your less admirable characteristics.'

Claude Montefiore, the liberal Jewish student of the Christian Gospels, found that a large part of the teaching of Jesus was parallelled in the best Rabbinic writing of about the same period. But on this aspect of the work of Jesus he wrote:

> Here we meet a new and gracious characteristic of Jesus and to it there are no parallels in Rabbinic literature. On the contrary, a respected Rabbi and teacher would have avoided eating and sitting at table with people of ill repute. That a teacher should go about and associate with such persons, and attempt to help and 'cure' them by friendly intercourse was, I imagine, an unheard of procedure. According to the Rabbis, the visiting of the *bodily* sick was an obligation of the first order. But the seeking out of the *morally* sick was not put on the same footing, nor, so far as we can gather, was it practised. Here Jesus appears to be 'original'. The great significance and importance of this new departure and its consequences are obvious.[10]

Nor was this all. When, as he foresaw, all the forces of respectability and priestly authority and imperial power and mob hysteria rose against him, he neither fought nor ran away. The decision against the use of force may not seem very impressive even though some of the Zealots must have hoped that Jesus would inspire an insurrection

[10] *Rabbinic Literature and Gospel Teaching* (Macmillan 1930), p. 272.

comparable to the gallant fight put up by the Maccabees some two hundred years earlier. But it can be said to have needed little more than common sense — perhaps even backed by timidity — to see the futility of an armed revolt against Rome. His other decision is rather different. Thousands of men and women — some of them previously judged to be quite ordinary — have shown amazing courage after being captured by their political or national enemies. But almost all of these have done their very best to avoid capture for as long as escape seemed possible. Not so, Jesus. After what would not then have been the Last Supper, he and his disciples had only to walk out of Jerusalem and go back to Galilee. No one would have stopped them. For many years the authorities would have allowed Jesus to preach his message to whatever crowds or groups he could collect in the northern kingdom. It was his presence and his challenge *in Jerusalem* that they found so intolerable. Even as little as half an hour before his arrest, Jesus could have stayed free if he had quietly led his disciples out of the Garden of Gethsemane. But he did not do it.

In this connection, five verses from St John's Gospel seem particularly impressive:

> And there were certain Greeks among them which came up to worship at the feast; the same came therefore to Philip which was of Bethsaida in Galilee and desired him saying, 'Sir, we would see Jesus.' Philip cometh and telleth Andrew; and again Andrew and Philip tell Jesus. And Jesus answered them saying, 'The hour is come that the Son of Man should be glorified. Verily, verily, I say unto you, except a corn of wheat fall into the ground and die, it abideth alone; but if it die, it bringeth forth much fruit.[11]

Could this episode create itself in the mouth-to-ear process that went on between the events and the first written

[11] John 12. 20–24.

record? Would the excited followers of Jesus have invented the thunderous reply to what looks like a very small request? And who were these Greeks? Those whose direct ancestors had heard the classical Greek philosophers would never have attended what they would have regarded as a sordid little festival among uneducated tribesmen. These were Hellenised Jews of the dispersion whose remaining faith brought them back to Jerusalem for the most important event in the Jewish year. Probably their dress and bearing distinguished them from local people who called them 'Greeks'.

And what of the fact that Philip went to consult Andrew who was, after all, one of the first two who ever committed themselves to Jesus?[12] Is this invented later by excited followers? It is not. It is in the record because the sequence of events fixed itself in the mind of at least one of the disciples who all understood, within a week, the significance of the answer that was given. And what did those 'Greeks' really want? They approached Philip on the first of three days in Jerusalem when Jesus was meeting every questioner and heckler that the city could provide. If these Hellenised Jews had wanted only to set eyes on Jesus and ask a few questions, it is inconceivable that he would have refused. Nor would Philip have bothered to consult Andrew. They wanted far more than a quick question-and-answer. 'Sir, *we* would see Jesus.' *We*, Hellenised Jews from Athens, want to see this debater in the intellectual centre of the world. It would have been a bright feather in the Jewish cap if they could have brought back, from their despised homeland, a man of the power and magnetism of Jesus. Beyond doubt they could have managed and financed it if Jesus had agreed. And if he had put his agreement onto the Jerusalem grape vine, he could have died a natural death and none of us would have heard of him. Very few would turn down the chance of a lecture tour in Greece for inevitable and immediate and total defeat on the gallows.

[12] John 7. 35–40.